MW01253321

TABLE OF CONTENTS

Top 20 Test Taking Tips

1. Carefully follow all the test registration procedures
2. Know the test directions, duration, topics, question types, how many questions
3. Setup a flexible study schedule at least 3-4 weeks before test day
4. Study during the time of day you are most alert, relaxed, and stress free
5. Maximize your learning style; visual learner use visual study aids, auditory learner use auditory study aids
6. Focus on your weakest knowledge base
7. Find a study partner to review with and help clarify questions
8. Practice, practice, practice
9. Get a good night's sleep; don't try to cram the night before the test
10. Eat a well balanced meal
11. Know the exact physical location of the testing site; drive the route to the site prior to test day
12. Bring a set of ear plugs; the testing center could be noisy
13. Wear comfortable, loose fitting, layered clothing to the testing center; prepare for it to be either cold or hot during the test
14. Bring at least 2 current forms of ID to the testing center
15. Arrive to the test early; be prepared to wait and be patient
16. Eliminate the obviously wrong answer choices, then guess the first remaining choice
17. Pace yourself; don't rush, but keep working and move on if you get stuck
18. Maintain a positive attitude even if the test is going poorly
19. Keep your first answer unless you are positive it is wrong
20. Check your work, don't make a careless mistake

Verbal Review

Rule Busters

Each problem provides you with some known information. These are the rules that you have to work with. Rule busters are choices that immediately clash with a rule and can be quickly ruled out.
Example:
John is sitting next to Bob.
This is a rule. Therefore any seating combination that does not have John sitting next to Bob is a rule buster, and is wrong! Quickly scan through the list of answer choices and eliminate all of those that have Bob and John sitting apart.

Example:
Mary is not sitting next to Bob.
Here is another rule. Quickly scan back through the answer choices and eliminate any that have Mary and Bob sitting together. For every rule that is given, quickly check and see if there are any answer choices that immediately "bust" the rule and eliminate them.

Symbology

Don't try to remember all of the information in your head. Sketch out the problem using the information provided. As much as possible, use symbols to represent the problem. Letters are great for abbreviation. Use a "M" as a symbol for a man, and a "W" as a symbol for a woman. Use the first letters in names to describe people. Therefore, John becomes "J" and Paul becomes "P". If the problem involves a seating or standing arrangement, use blanks to represent the possible seats. Then if a rule states that John is in the rightmost seat, put a "J" in the rightmost blank. Fill in as much information as you can using your symbols. Symbols will help you save time from writing the names out and will allow you to make fast and accurate diagrams of the problem.

Scratch Aides

Use your text booklet as scratch paper extensively. It's a great ally! If you finish the Analytical Reasoning section without scribbles throughout, you didn't take advantage of all of your potential resources. A good diagram or drawing of the problem described gives you a huge aid to solving the problem. Take advantage of it!

Be forewarned though, when creating your drawings, be efficient. Don't waste time filling in more information that you need. This is why symbols are great tools. They will save time and effort. Don't include useless information on your diagram or spend time making it "pretty". Fill in what you can quickly deduce. Focus on getting the bare essentials down on paper and spend your time more productively trying to solve the problem.

Tough Questions

If you are stumped on a problem or it appears too hard or too difficult, don't waste time. Move on! Remember though, if you can quickly check for obvious "rule busters" your chances of guessing correctly are greatly improved. Before you completely give up, at least check for the easy rule busters, which should knock out a couple of possible answers. Eliminate what you can and then guess at the remainder before moving on.

Face Value

Always accept the situation in the problem at face value. Don't read too much into it. The Wonderlic isn't trying to throw you off with a cheap trick. If it says there are six seats in a row, you can be confident that it is a single file row and one person is seated directly beside the next person and there are two ends to the row. Don't overcomplicate the problem by creating theoretical scenarios that will warp time or space. These are normal problems with solvable answers. It's just that all of the information isn't readily apparent and you have to figure things out.

Read Carefully

Understand what the problem is about. Read the description of the problem carefully. Don't miss the question because you misunderstood the explanation of the problem. The description is there because it is important in understanding the problem. Don't waste too much time though. You must read carefully and efficiently.

Danger Words

Some words go with a warning. They can be dangerous in any problem, not just Analytical Reasoning problems. These are "hedge" words such as the following: only, exactly, but, never, can be, cannot be, always, must be, least, most, highest, lowest, first, last, none, entire, all, no, unless, each, every. These words can completely alter the meaning of a sentence or a question and can easily be missed if you're reading quickly. Watch out!

Loose vs Tight

Rules are often either "loose" or "tight". Don't confuse the two when you check for rule breakers. A loose rule gives vague details about the problem. A tight rule gives specific details about the problem. Tight rules are much more helpful, providing more information, and allowing you to make clear determinations about answer choices more easily.
Example:
Loose: Bob is standing somewhere behind Joe.
Tight: Bob is standing directly behind Joe.
Don't mistakenly eliminate an answer choice that has Bob standing two spaces back from Joe, if only the loose rule above is given. If the loose rule is given, you can only eliminate answer choices that have Bob in front of Joe.

Double Negatives

A double negative can be treated as an affirmative. If a rule or answer choice has two negatives, mentally switch it to a single positive.
Example:
He is not going to not be there. = He is going to be there.

Answer Selection

Eliminate choices as soon as you realize they are wrong. But be careful! Make sure you consider all of the possible answer choices. Just because one appears right, doesn't mean that the next one won't be even better! Take a second to make sure that the other choices are not equally obvious. Don't make a hasty mistake. There are only two times that you should stop before checking other answers. First is when you are positive that the answer choice you have selected satisfies all of the rules. Second is when time is almost out and you have to make a quick guess!

The Wonderlic test will usually put more than one good answer choice for every question, so read all of them. Don't worry if you are stuck between two that seem right. By eliminating the other three your odds are now 50/50 if you have it down to two. Rather than wasting too much time, play the odds. You are guessing, but guessing wisely, because you've been able to knock out some of the answer choices that you know are wrong. If you are eliminating choices and realize that the answer choice you are left with is also obviously wrong, don't panic. Start over and consider each choice again. There may easily be something that you missed the first time and will realize on the second pass.

Common Sense

When in doubt, use common sense. These problems will not require you to make huge leaps of logic. If you think a leap of logic is necessary, read back through the set of conditions and question in order to gain a better understanding. Don't read too much into the question or set of conditions. Use your common sense to interpret anything that isn't clear. These are normal problems rooted in reality.

Final Notes

Some problems may have complicated reasoning that must be sorted through. Before you pick an answer choice and work it out in great detail, which takes a lot of time, first look briefly through the other answer choices to see if any of them are readily obvious as being correct. Always use your time efficiently. Don't panic, stay focused. Work systematically. Read the problem carefully. Eliminate the answer choices that are immediately wrong and are rule busters. Keep narrowing the search until you are either left with the answer or must guess at the answer from a more selective group of choices.

Mathematics Review

Most of the math problems on the Wonderlic are in the form of word problems. With word problems, the difficulty is rarely in performing the calculations themselves. Instead, the difficulty is in determining what calculations need to be performed, which typically involves translating the word problem into an equation or set of equations. The following sections will go over the computation skills and concepts you'll need for the test, but the more important skill is speed in interpreting the word problems. For that, there's nothing that will substitute for lots of practice.

Numbers and their Classifications

Numbers are the basic building blocks of mathematics. Specific features of numbers are identified by the following terms:

Integers – The set of whole positive and negative numbers, including zero. Integers do not include fractions $\left(\frac{1}{3}\right)$, decimals (0.56), or mixed numbers $\left(7\frac{3}{4}\right)$.

Prime number – A whole number greater than 1 that has only two factors, itself and 1; that is, a number that can be divided evenly only by 1 and itself.

Composite number – A whole number greater than 1 that has more than two different factors; in other words, any whole number that is not a prime number. For example: The composite number 8 has the factors of 1, 2, 4, and 8.

Even number – Any integer that can be divided by 2 without leaving a remainder. For example: 2, 4, 6, 8, and so on.

Odd number – Any integer that cannot be divided evenly by 2. For example: 3, 5, 7, 9, and so on.

Decimal number – a number that uses a decimal point to show the part of the number that is less than one. Example: 1.234.

Decimal point – a symbol used to separate the ones place from the tenths place in decimals or dollars from cents in currency.

Decimal place – the position of a number to the right of the decimal point. In the decimal 0.123, the 1 is in the first place to the right of the decimal point, indicating tenths; the 2 is in the second place, indicating hundredths; and the 3 is in the third place, indicating thousandths.

The decimal, or base 10, system is a number system that uses ten different digits (0, 1, 2, 3, 4, 5, 6, 7, 8, 9). An example of a number system that uses something other than ten digits is the binary, or base 2, number system, used by computers, which uses only the numbers 0 and 1. It is thought that the decimal system originated because people had only their 10 fingers for counting.

Rational, irrational, and real numbers can be described as follows:
Rational numbers include all integers, decimals, and fractions. Any terminating or repeating decimal number is a rational number.
Irrational numbers cannot be written as fractions or decimals because the number of decimal places is infinite and there is no recurring pattern of digits within the number. For

example, pi (π) begins with 3.141592 and continues without terminating or repeating, so pi is an irrational number.

Real numbers are the set of all rational and irrational numbers.

> **Review Video: Numbers and Their Classification**
> *Visit mometrix.com/academy and enter Code:* **461071**

Operations

There are four basic mathematical operations:

Addition increases the value of one quantity by the value of another quantity. Example: $2 + 4 = 6; 8 + 9 = 17$. The result is called the sum. With addition, the order does not matter. $4 + 2 = 2 + 4$.

Subtraction is the opposite operation to addition; it decreases the value of one quantity by the value of another quantity. Example: $6 - 4 = 2; 17 - 8 = 9$. The result is called the difference. Note that with subtraction, the order does matter. $6 - 4 \neq 4 - 6$.

> **Review Video: Addition and Subtraction**
> *Visit mometrix.com/academy and enter Code:* **521157**

Multiplication can be thought of as repeated addition. One number tells how many times to add the other number to itself. Example: 3×2 (three times two) $= 2 + 2 + 2 = 6$. With multiplication, the order does not matter. $2 \times 3 = 3 \times 2$ or $3 + 3 = 2 + 2 + 2$.

Division is the opposite operation to multiplication; one number tells us how many parts to divide the other number into. Example: $20 \div 4 = 5$; if 20 is split into 4 equal parts, each part is 5. With division, the order of the numbers does matter. $20 \div 4 \neq 4 \div 20$.

> **Review Video: Multiplication and Division**
> *Visit mometrix.com/academy and enter Code:* **643326**

An exponent is a superscript number placed next to another number at the top right. It indicates how many times the base number is to be multiplied by itself. Exponents provide a shorthand way to write what would be a longer mathematical expression. Example: $a^2 = a \times a; 2^4 = 2 \times 2 \times 2 \times 2$. A number with an exponent of 2 is said to be "squared," while a number with an exponent of 3 is said to be "cubed." The value of a number raised to an exponent is called its power. So, 8^4 is read as "8 to the 4th power," or "8 raised to the power of 4." A negative exponent is the same as the reciprocal of a positive exponent. Example: $a^{-2} = \frac{1}{a^2}$.

> **Review Video: Exponents**
> *Visit mometrix.com/academy and enter Code:* **600998**

Parentheses are used to designate which operations should be done first when there are multiple operations. Example: $4 - (2 + 1) = 1$; the parentheses tell us that we must add 2

- 10 -

and 1, and then subtract the sum from 4, rather than subtracting 2 from 4 and then adding 1 (this would give us an answer of 3).

Order of Operations is a set of rules that dictates the order in which we must perform each operation in an expression so that we will evaluate at accurately. If we have an expression that includes multiple different operations, Order of Operations tells us which operations to do first. The most common mnemonic for Order of Operations is PEMDAS, or "Please Excuse My Dear Aunt Sally." PEMDAS stands for Parentheses, Exponents, Multiplication, Division, Addition, Subtraction. It is important to understand that multiplication and division have equal precedence, as do addition and subtraction, so those pairs of operations are simply worked from left to right in order.

Example: Evaluate the expression $5 + 20 \div 4 \times (2 + 3)^2 - 6$ using the correct order of operations.

P: Perform the operations inside the parentheses, $(2 + 3) = 5$.

E: Simplify the exponents, $(5)^2 = 25$.

The equation now looks like this: $5 + 20 \div 4 \times 25 - 6$.

MD: Perform multiplication and division from left to right, $20 \div 4 = 5$; then $5 \times 25 = 125$. The equation now looks like this: $5 + 125 - 6$.

AS: Perform addition and subtraction from left to right, $5 + 125 = 130$; then $130 - 6 = 124$.

> **Review Video: Order of Operations**
Visit mometrix.com/academy and enter Code: **259675**

The laws of exponents are as follows:

1)	Any number to the power of 1 is equal to itself: $a^1 = a$.
2)	The number 1 raised to any power is equal to 1: $1^n = 1$.
3)	Any number raised to the power of 0 is equal to 1: $a^0 = 1$.
4)	Add exponents to multiply powers of the same base number:$a^n \times a^m = a^{n+m}$.
5)	Subtract exponents to divide powers of the same number; that is $a^n \div a^m = a^{n-m}$.
6)	Multiply exponents to raise a power to a power: $(a^n)^m = a^{n \times m}$.
7)	If multiplied or divided numbers inside parentheses are collectively raised to a power, this is the same as each individual term being raised to that power: $(a \times b)^n = a^n \times b^n$; $(a \div b)^n = a^n \div b^n$.

Note: Exponents do not have to be integers. Fractional or decimal exponents follow all the rules above as well. Example: $5^{\frac{1}{4}} \times 5^{\frac{3}{4}} = 5^{\frac{1}{4}+\frac{3}{4}} = 5^1 = 5$.

A root, such as a square root, is another way of writing a fractional exponent. Instead of using a superscript, roots use the radical symbol ($\sqrt{}$) to indicate the operation. A radical will have a number underneath the bar, and may sometimes have a number in the upper left: $\sqrt[n]{a}$, read as "the nth root of a." The relationship between radical notation and exponent notation can be described by this equation: $\sqrt[n]{a} = a^{\frac{1}{n}}$. The two special cases of $n = 2$ and $n = 3$ are called square roots and cube roots. If there is no number to the upper left, it is understood to be a square root ($n = 2$). Nearly all of the roots you encounter will be square roots. A square root is the same as a number raised to the one-half power. When we say that a is the square root of b ($a = \sqrt{b}$), we mean that a multiplied by itself equals b: ($a \times a = b$).

- 11 -

A perfect square is a number that has an integer for its square root. There are 10 perfect squares from 1 to 100: 1, 4, 9, 16, 25, 36, 49, 64, 81, 100 (the squares of integers 1 through 10).

> ➢ **Review Video:** <u>Square Root and Perfect Square</u>
> *Visit **mometrix.com/academy** and enter **Code: 648063***

Scientific notation is a way of writing large numbers in a shorter form. The form $a \times 10^n$ is used in scientific notation, where a is greater than or equal to 1, but less than 10, and n is the number of places the decimal must move to get from the original number to a. Example: The number 230,400,000 is cumbersome to write. To write the value in scientific notation, place a decimal point between the first and second numbers, and include all digits through the last non-zero digit ($a = 2.304$). To find the appropriate power of 10, count the number of places the decimal point had to move ($n = 8$). The number is positive if the decimal moved to the left, and negative if it moved to the right. We can then write 230,400,000 as 2.304×10^8. If we look instead at the number 0.00002304, we have the same value for a, but this time the decimal moved 5 places to the right ($n = -5$). Thus, 0.00002304 can be written as 2.304×10^{-5}. Using this notation makes it simple to compare very large or very small numbers. By comparing exponents, it is easy to see that 3.28×10^4 is smaller than 1.51×10^5, because 4 is less than 5.

> ➢ **Review Video:** <u>Scientific Notation</u>
> *Visit **mometrix.com/academy** and enter **Code: 976454***

Positive and Negative Numbers

A precursor to working with negative numbers is understanding what absolute values are. A number's *Absolute Value* is simply the distance away from zero a number is on the number line. The absolute value of a number is always positive and is written $|x|$.

When adding signed numbers, if the signs are the same simply add the absolute values of the addends and apply the original sign to the sum. For example, $(+4) + (+8) = +12$ and $(-4) + (-8) = -12$. When the original signs are different, take the absolute values of the addends and subtract the smaller value from the larger value, then apply the original sign of the larger value to the difference. For instance, $(+4) + (-8) = -4$ and $(-4) + (+8) = +4$.

For subtracting signed numbers, change the sign of the number after the minus symbol and then follow the same rules used for addition. For example, $(+4) - (+8) = (+4) + (-8) = -4$.

If the signs are the same the product is positive when multiplying signed numbers. For example, $(+4) \times (+8) = +32$ and $(-4) \times (-8) = +32$. If the signs are opposite, the product is negative. For example, $(+4) \times (-8) = -32$ and $(-4) \times (+8) = -32$. When more than two factors are multiplied together, the sign of the product is determined by how many negative factors are present. If there are an odd number of negative factors then the product is negative, whereas an even number of negative factors indicates a positive product. For instance, $(+4) \times (-8) \times (-2) = +64$ and $(-4) \times (-8) \times (-2) = -64$.

The rules for dividing signed numbers are similar to multiplying signed numbers. If the dividend and divisor have the same sign, the quotient is positive. If the dividend and divisor have opposite signs, the quotient is negative. For example, $(-4) \div (+8) = -0.5$.

Factors and Multiples

Factors are numbers that are multiplied together to obtain a product. For example, in the equation $2 \times 3 = 6$, the numbers 2 and 3 are factors. A prime number has only two factors (1 and itself), but other numbers can have many factors.
A common factor is a number that divides exactly into two or more other numbers. For example, the factors of 12 are 1, 2, 3, 4, 6, and 12, while the factors of 15 are 1, 3, 5, and 15. The common factors of 12 and 15 are 1 and 3.
A prime factor is also a prime number. Therefore, the prime factors of 12 are 2 and 3. For 15, the prime factors are 3 and 5.

> ➢ **Review Video: <u>Factors</u>**
> *Visit **mometrix.com/academy** and enter **Code: 920086***

The greatest common factor (GCF) is the largest number that is a factor of two or more numbers. For example, the factors of 15 are 1, 3, 5, and 15; the factors of 35 are 1, 5, 7, and 35. Therefore, the greatest common factor of 15 and 35 is 5.

> ➢ **Review Video: <u>Greatest Common Factor</u>**
> *Visit **mometrix.com/academy** and enter **Code: 838699***

The least common multiple (LCM) is the smallest number that is a multiple of two or more numbers. For example, the multiples of 3 include 3, 6, 9, 12, 15, etc.; the multiples of 5 include 5, 10, 15, 20, etc. Therefore, the least common multiple of 3 and 5 is 15.

> ➢ **Review Video: <u>Least Common Multiple</u>**
> *Visit **mometrix.com/academy** and enter **Code: 946579***

Fractions, Percentages, and Related Concepts

A fraction is a number that is expressed as one integer written above another integer, with a dividing line between them $(\frac{x}{y})$. It represents the quotient of the two numbers "x divided by y." It can also be thought of as x out of y equal parts.

The top number of a fraction is called the numerator, and it represents the number of parts under consideration. The 1 in $\frac{1}{4}$ means that 1 part out of the whole is being considered in the calculation. The bottom number of a fraction is called the denominator, and it

- 13 -

represents the total number of equal parts. The 4 in $\frac{1}{4}$ means that the whole consists of 4 equal parts. A fraction cannot have a denominator of zero; this is referred to as "undefined."

> ➤ **Review Video:** <u>Fractions</u>
> Visit **mometrix.com/academy** and enter **Code: 262335**

Fractions can be manipulated, without changing the value of the fraction, by multiplying or dividing (but not adding or subtracting) both the numerator and denominator by the same number. If you divide both numbers by a common factor, you are reducing or simplifying the fraction. Two fractions that have the same value, but are expressed differently are known as equivalent fractions. For example, $\frac{2}{10}, \frac{3}{15}, \frac{4}{20}$, and $\frac{5}{25}$ are all equivalent fractions. They can also all be reduced or simplified to $\frac{1}{5}$.

When two fractions are manipulated so that they have the same denominator, this is known as finding a common denominator. The number chosen to be that common denominator should be the least common multiple of the two original denominators. Example: $\frac{3}{4}$ and $\frac{5}{6}$; the least common multiple of 4 and 6 is 12. Manipulating to achieve the common denominator: $\frac{3}{4} = \frac{9}{12}; \frac{5}{6} = \frac{10}{12}$.

If two fractions have a common denominator, they can be added or subtracted simply by adding or subtracting the two numerators and retaining the same denominator. Example: $\frac{1}{2} + \frac{1}{4} = \frac{2}{4} + \frac{1}{4} = \frac{3}{4}$. If the two fractions do not already have the same denominator, one or both of them must be manipulated to achieve a common denominator before they can be added or subtracted.

> ➤ **Review Video:** <u>Adding and Subtracting Fractions</u>
> Visit **mometrix.com/academy** and enter **Code: 378080**

Two fractions can be multiplied by multiplying the two numerators to find the new numerator and the two denominators to find the new denominator. Example: $\frac{1}{3} \times \frac{2}{3} = \frac{1 \times 2}{3 \times 3} = \frac{2}{9}$.

> ➤ **Review Video:** <u>Multiplying Fractions</u>
> Visit **mometrix.com/academy** and enter **Code: 638849**

Two fractions can be divided flipping the numerator and denominator of the second fraction and then proceeding as though it were a multiplication. Example: $\frac{2}{3} \div \frac{3}{4} = \frac{2}{3} \times \frac{4}{3} = \frac{8}{9}$.

> ➤ **Review Video:** <u>Dividing Fractions</u>
> Visit **mometrix.com/academy** and enter **Code: 300874**

A fraction whose denominator is greater than its numerator is known as a proper fraction, while a fraction whose numerator is greater than its denominator is known as an improper fraction. Proper fractions have values less than one and improper fractions have values greater than one.

- 14 -

A mixed number is a number that contains both an integer and a fraction. Any improper fraction can be rewritten as a mixed number. Example: $\frac{8}{3} = \frac{6}{3} + \frac{2}{3} = 2 + \frac{2}{3} = 2\frac{2}{3}$. Similarly, any mixed number can be rewritten as an improper fraction. Example: $1\frac{3}{5} = 1 + \frac{3}{5} = \frac{5}{5} + \frac{3}{5} = \frac{8}{5}$.

Percentages can be thought of as fractions that are based on a whole of 100; that is, one whole is equal to 100%. The word percent means "per hundred." Fractions can be expressed as percents by finding equivalent fractions with a denomination of 100. Example: $\frac{7}{10} = \frac{70}{100} = 70\%$; $\frac{1}{4} = \frac{25}{100} = 25\%$.

> ➤ **Review Video: Percentages**
> *Visit mometrix.com/academy and enter Code:* **141911**

To express a percentage as a fraction, divide the percentage number by 100 and reduce the fraction to its simplest possible terms. Example: $60\% = \frac{60}{100} = \frac{3}{5}$; $96\% = \frac{96}{100} = \frac{24}{25}$.

Converting decimals to percentages and percentages to decimals is as simple as moving the decimal point. To convert from a decimal to a percent, move the decimal point two places to the right. To convert from a percent to a decimal, move it two places to the left. Example: 0.23 = 23%; 5.34 = 534%; 0.007 = 0.7%; 700% = 7.00; 86% = 0.86; 0.15% = 0.0015. It may be helpful to remember that the percentage number will always be larger than the equivalent decimal number.

> ➤ **Review Video: Converting Decimals to Fractions and Percentages**
> *Visit mometrix.com/academy and enter Code:* **986765**

A percentage problem can be presented three main ways:
- Find what percentage of some number another number is.
  Example: What percentage of 40 is 8?
- Find what number is some percentage of a given number.
  Example: What number is 20% of 40?
- Find what number another number is a given percentage of.
  Example: What number is 8 20% of?

The three components in all of these cases are the same: a whole (W), a part (P), and a percentage (%). These are related by the equation: $P = W \times \%$. This is the form of the equation you would use to solve problems of type (2). To solve types (1) and (3), you would use these two forms: $\% = \frac{P}{W}$ and $W = \frac{P}{\%}$.

The thing that frequently makes percentage problems difficult is that they are most often also word problems, so a large part of solving them is figuring out which quantities are what. Example: In a school cafeteria, 7 students choose pizza, 9 choose hamburgers, and 4 choose tacos. Find the percentage that chooses tacos. To find the whole, you must first add all of the parts: 7 + 9 + 4 = 20. The percentage can then be found by dividing the part by the whole (% = $\frac{P}{W}$): $\frac{4}{20} = \frac{20}{100}$ = 20%.

A ratio is a comparison of two quantities in a particular order. Example: If there are 14 computers in a lab, and the class has 20 students, there is a student to computer ratio of 20 to 14, commonly written as 20:14. Ratios are normally reduced to their smallest whole number representation, so 20:14 would be reduced to 10:7 by dividing both sides by 2.

> **Review Video: Ratios**
Visit mometrix.com/academy and enter Code: **996914**

A proportion is a relationship between two quantities that dictates how one changes when the other changes. A direct proportion describes a relationship in which a quantity increases by a set amount for every increase in the other quantity, or decreases by that same amount for every decrease in the other quantity. Example: Assuming a constant driving speed, the time required for a car trip increases as the distance of the trip increases. The distance to be traveled and the time required to travel are directly proportional.

> **Review Video: Proportions**
Visit mometrix.com/academy and enter Code: **505355**

Inverse proportion is a relationship in which an increase in one quantity is accompanied by a decrease in the other, or vice versa. Example: the time required for a car trip decreases as the speed increases, and increases as the speed decreases, so the time required is inversely proportional to the speed of the car.

Systems of Equations

Systems of Equations are a set of simultaneous equations that all use the same variables. A solution to a system of equations must be true for each equation in the system. *Consistent Systems* are those with at least one solution. *Inconsistent Systems* are systems of equations that have no solution.

To solve a system of linear equations by *substitution*, start with the easier equation and solve for one of the variables. Express this variable in terms of the other variable. Substitute this expression in the other equation, and solve for the other variable. The solution should be expressed in the form (x, y). Substitute the values into both of the original equations to check your answer. Consider the following problem.

Solve the system using substitution:
$$x + 6y = 15$$
$$3x - 12y = 18$$

Solve the first equation for x:
$$x = 15 - 6y$$

Substitute this value in place of x in the second equation, and solve for y:
$$3(15 - 6y) - 12y = 18$$
$$45 - 18y - 12y = 18$$
$$30y = 27$$
$$y = \frac{27}{30} = \frac{9}{10} = 0.9$$

Plug this value for y back into the first equation to solve for x:
$$x = 15 - 6(0.9) = 15 - 5.4 = 9.6$$

Check both equations if you have time:
$$9.6 + 6(0.9) = 9.6 + 5.4 = 15$$
$$3(9.6) - 12(0.9) = 28.8 - 10.8 = 18$$
Therefore, the solution is $(9.6, 0.9)$.

To solve a system of equations using *elimination*, begin by rewriting both equations in standard form $Ax + By = C$. Check to see if the coefficients of one pair of like variables add to zero. If not, multiply one or both of the equations by a non-zero number to make one set of like variables add to zero. Add the two equations to solve for one of the variables. Substitute this value into one of the original equations to solve for the other variable. Check your work by substituting into the other equation. Next we will solve the same problem as above, but using the addition method.

Solve the system using elimination:
$$x + 6y = 15$$
$$3x - 12y = 18$$

If we multiply the first equation by 2, we can eliminate the y terms:
$$2x + 12y = 30$$
$$3x - 12y = 18$$

Add the equations together and solve for x:
$$5x = 48$$
$$x = \frac{48}{5} = 9.6$$

Plug the value for x back into either of the original equations and solve for y:
$$9.6 + 6y = 15$$
$$y = \frac{15 - 9.6}{6} = 0.9$$

Check both equations if you have time:
$$9.6 + 6(0.9) = 9.6 + 5.4 = 15$$
$$3(9.6) - 12(0.9) = 28.8 - 10.8 = 18$$
Therefore, the solution is (9.6, 0.9).

➢ **Review Video: System of Equations**
*Visit **mometrix.com/academy** and enter **Code**: 658153*

Polynomial Algebra

To multiply two binomials, follow the *FOIL* method. FOIL stands for:
- First: Multiply the first term of each binomial
- Outer: Multiply the outer terms of each binomial
- Inner: Multiply the inner terms of each binomial
- Last: Multiply the last term of each binomial

Using FOIL, $(Ax + By)(Cx + Dy) = ACx^2 + ADxy + BCxy + BDy^2$.

➢ **Review Video: Multiplying Terms Using the Foil Method**
*Visit **mometrix.com/academy** and enter **Code**: 854792*

Special Report: Wonderlic Secrets in Action

Sample Math Question:

Three coins are tossed up in the air. What is the probability that two of them will land heads and one will land tails?

A. 0
B. 1/8
C. 1/4
D. 3/8

Let's look at a few different methods and steps to solving this problem.

1. Reduction and Division

Quickly eliminate the probabilities that you immediately know. You know to roll all heads is a 1/8 probability, and to roll all tails is a 1/8 probability. Since there are in total 8/8 probabilities, you can subtract those two out, leaving you with 8/8 – 1/8 – 1/8 = 6/8. So after eliminating the possibilities of getting all heads or all tails, you're left with 6/8 probability. Because there are only three coins, all other combinations are going to involve one of either head or tail, and two of the other. All other combinations will either be 2 heads and 1 tail, or 2 tails and 1 head. Those remaining combinations both have the same chance of occurring, meaning that you can just cut the remaining 6/8 probability in half, leaving you with a 3/8ths chance that there will be 2 heads and 1 tail, and another 3/8ths chance that there will be 2 tails and 1 head, making choice D correct.

2. Run Through the Possibilities for that Outcome
You know that you have to have two heads and one tail for the three coins. There are only so many combinations, so quickly run through them all.

You could have:
H, H, H
H, H, T
H, T, H
T, H, H
T, T, H
T, H, T
H, T, T
T, T, T

Reviewing these choices, you can see that three of the eight have two heads and one tail, making choice D correct.

3. Fill in the Blanks with Symbology and Odds

Many probability problems can be solved by drawing blanks on a piece of scratch paper (or making mental notes) for each object used in the problem, then filling in probabilities and multiplying them out. In this case, since there are three coins being flipped, draw three blanks. In the first blank, put an "H" and over it write "1/2". This represents the case where the first coin is flipped as heads. In that case (where the first coin comes up heads), one of the other two coins must come up tails and one must come up heads to fulfill the criteria posed in the problem (2 heads and 1 tail). In the second blank, put a "1" or "1/1". This is because it doesn't matter what is flipped for the second coin, so long as the first coin is heads. In the third blank, put a "1/2". This is because the third coin must be the exact opposite of whatever is in the second blank. Half the time the third coin will be the same as the second coin, and half the time the third coin will be the opposite, hence the "1/2". Now multiply out the odds. There is a half chance that the first coin will come up "heads", then it doesn't matter for the second coin, then there is a half chance that the third coin will be the opposite of the second coin, which will give the desired result of 2 heads and 1 tail. So, that gives 1/2*1/1*1/2 = 1/4.

But, now you must calculate the probabilities that result if the first coin is flipped tails. So draw another group of three blanks. In the first blank, put a "T" and over it write "1/2". This represents the case where the first coin is flipped as tails. In that case (where the first coin comes up tails), both of the other two coins must come up heads to fulfill the criteria posed in the problem. In the second blank, put an "H" and over it write "1/2". In the third blank, put an "H" and over it write "1/2". Now multiply out the odds. There is a half chance that the first coin will come up "tails", then there is a half chance that the second coin will be heads, and a half chance that the third coin will be heads. So, that gives 1/2*1/2*1/2 = 1/8.

Now, add those two probabilities together. If you flip heads with the first coin, there is a 1/4 chance of ultimately meeting the problem's criteria. If you flip tails with the first coin, there is a 1/8 chance of ultimately meeting the problem's criteria. So, that gives 1/4 + 1/8 = 2/8 + 1/8 = 3/8, which makes choice D correct.

Practice Test #1

Practice Questions

1.   REFRAIN   RECUSE
These words have:
    a. Similar meanings
    b. Contradictory meanings
    c. Neither similar nor contradictory meanings

2. Look at the row of numbers below. What number should come next?
        10   20   15   30   25   50   ?
    a. 35
    b. 40
    c. 45
    d. 100

3. Assume the first two statements are true.
    1. The girl plays outside every day
    2. The weather is sometimes snowy
    3. The girl is sometimes snowed upon

The third statement is:
    a. True
    b. False
    c. Not certain

4. If it takes 1.5 hours to fly from city A to city B, and it takes 9 hours to fly from city A to city C, how much greater is the distance between cities A and C than the distance between cities A and B?
    a. Two times as great
    b. Four times as great
    c. Six times as great
    d. Seven-and-a-half times as great

5. If the first day of May is a Friday, what day will the 27th fall on?
    a. Tuesday
    b. Wednesday
    c. Thursday
    d. Friday

6. How many of the five pairs of names listed below are exact duplicates?

M.K. Fisher	M.K. Fischer
J.S. Waters	J.C. Waters
A.C. Thule	A.C. Thule
E.L. Petersen	E.L. Peterson
L.B. Baird	L.B. Baird

7. Owen and James start work at a company at the same time. Owen earns twice as much as James at first, but he does not receive a raise for five years, while James receives a $5,000 raise every year. After five years, their salaries are equal. How much did James make when they started working?
   a. $5,000
   b. $25,000
   c. $50,000
   d. $100,000

8.   RETRACT   RETRIEVE
These words have:
   a. Similar meanings
   b. Contradictory meanings
   c. Neither similar nor contradictory meanings

9. Look at the row of numbers below. Which number is the smallest?

   2   0.2   1/2   0.02   1/20

10. Lumber is on sale for 50% off the regular price. Rebecca purchases 5 meters of lumber for $12.50. What is the regular price per meter of lumber?
   a. $2.50
   b. $5.00
   c. $15.00
   d. $17.50

11.   REPORT   REPRESS
These words have:
   a. Similar meanings
   b. Contradictory meanings
   c. Neither similar nor contradictory meanings

12. The numbers in the figures below have the same mathematical relationship to one another.

What number should replace the question mark in the figure below?

   a. 0
   b. 2
   c. 6
   d. 10

13. Assume the following two statements are true:
      All students are required to take a math class before they graduate.
      Sharon is a student.

Which of the following statements could be logically concluded?
   a. Sharon is required to take a math class
   b. Sharon is not a student
   c. Sharon is not required to take a math class
   d. Sharon is currently taking a math class

14. Define the value of a word as the sum of all letters, if each letter is replaced by a number representing its position in the alphabet. For example, the value of "cab" is 6, because C (3) + A (1) + B (2) = 6.

What is the value of the word "egg"?
   a. 15
   b. 17
   c. 19
   d. 21

15. Which month of the year contains the *fewest* hours of daylight in the Northern Hemisphere?
    a. January
    b. July
    c. October
    d. December

16. Assume the first two statements are true.
        1. All employees must submit time sheets weekly
        2. Mike is an employee
        3. Mike has submitted this week's time sheet

The third statement is:
    a. True
    b. False
    c. Not certain

17. Widgets sell for 50 cents each, for sales of up to 2,000 widgets. After that, the price drops to 25 cents each for all sales of more than 2,000 widgets. A customer pays $1,500 for his widget order. How many widgets has he ordered?
    a. 1,000
    b. 2,000
    c. 3,000
    d. 4,000

18.   CONFOUND   CONFUSE
These words have:
    a. Similar meanings
    b. Contradictory meanings
    c. Neither similar nor contradictory meanings

19. Which of the following figures is most different from the others?
    a.   b.   c.   d.

20. A woman needs to replace the tires on her car. Brand A costs $500 and will last for 50,000 miles. Brand B costs $400 and will last for 40,000 miles. Which brand offers the best value based on miles per dollar?
   a. Brand A
   b. Brand B
   c. Both offer equal value

21. Which word does not fit in the following list?
   revive   resume   revert   renew

22. Look at the row of numbers below. Which number is the smallest?
   1/3   3   0.3   3/100   0.003

23. Assume the first two statements are true.
   1. Joe and Sally know one another
   2. Sally and Ian know one another
   3. Joe and Ian know one another

The third statement is:
   a. True
   b. False
   c. Not certain

24. Two people leave a city at the same time. One person travels at 30 miles an hour and arrives three hours later at his destination. The second person travels to a city 120 miles away and arrives at the same time. How fast is the second person traveling?
   a. 30 miles an hour
   b. 40 miles an hour
   c. 50 miles an hour
   d. 60 miles an hour

25. The officer cited the man for reckless driving, saying that he had failed to **heed** the signs about dangerous weather conditions.

In this context, **heed** most nearly means:
   a. Obey
   b. Ignore
   c. See

26. Which of the following words contains the greatest number of *different* letters?
   a. Abracadabra
   b. Onomatopoeia
   c. Disillusionment

- 25 -

27. A man is 1.5 times as old as his sister. He is now 30 years old. How old was he when she was born?
    a. 5
    b. 10
    c. 15
    d. 20

28. Which word does not fit in the following list?
        inspire   regret   outrage   provoke

29. Which of the following figures is most different from the others?
    a.   b.   c.   d.

30. Plants are sold for $6 each. If a customer buys more than ten plants, the price drops to $5 for each plant after the tenth. How much will a customer pay for 15 plants?
    a. $75
    b. $85
    c. $90
    d. $100

Answers and Explanations

1. A: have similar meanings. Both "to refrain" and "to recuse" refer to choosing not to participate in an activity.

2. C: The series of numbers is formed by performing two operations: doubling the first number to get the second, and then subtracting 5 to get the next, and repeating this pattern. Since 50 is 25 doubled, the next operation is to subtract 5, resulting in 45.

3. A: true. If the girl plays outside every day and the weather is sometimes snowy, then she will be playing outside on days it is snowy and will be snowed upon.

4. C: six times as far. Nine divided by 1.5 equals 6, so city C is six times farther from city A than city B is.

5. B: a Wednesday. There are seven days in a week, so adding multiples of 7 to 1 (for the first of the month) will find the other Fridays in the month. The other Fridays will be the 8th, the 15th, the 22nd, and the 29th. The 27th will be two days before Friday the 29th, meaning it will fall on a Wednesday.

6. Two are exact duplicates, A.C. Thule and L.B. Baird. In the first pair, Fisher is spelled differently from Fischer. In the second pair, the initials are J.S. and J.C. In the fourth pair, Petersen and Peterson are spelled differently.

7. B: $25,000. If James receives a $5,000 raise every year for five years, he has gained an income increase of $25,000. If their salaries are now equal, and James's salary was initially one-half of Owen's, then James has doubled his salary. Therefore, James initially earned $25,000.

8. A: have similar meanings. Both words involve taking something back; "to retract" something is to draw it back or withdraw it (for instance, a statement), and "to retrieve" something can mean to get it back or regain it.

9. 0.02. To find the answer, reformat all the numbers so they can be more easily compared. Since the list contains one fraction, change it to a decimal, and extend all numbers to two decimal places. Reformatting our list, we get

2.00   0.20   0.50   0.02   0.05

Now it is easy to see that 0.02 is the smallest number in the list.

10. B: $5.00. Rebecca purchased 5 meters of lumber for $12.50, so we simply divide $12.50 by 5 to find the sale price for one meter. 12.5 divided by 5 equals 2.5, so the sale price per meter is $2.50. The regular price is twice the sale price since the sale price is a 50% discount, so the regular price is $5.00 per meter.

11. B: have contradictory meanings. "To report" involves the disclosure of information, while "to repress" involves withholding it or preventing it from being disclosed.

12. D: 10. The numbers in the bottom boxes are exactly twice the number diagonal to them in the top boxes. In the example, 1 × 2 = 2 in the first figure, 2 × 2 = 4 and 3 × 2 = 6 in the second figure, and 0 × 2 = 0 and –1 × 2 = –2 in the third figure. In the question, we see that 3 × 2 = 6, just as in the example, so we should multiply 5 by 2 to get the missing answer, which is 10.

13. A: "Sharon is required to take a math class." B, "Sharon is not a student" is contradicted by the information we have already been given. C, "Sharon is not required to take a math class" cannot be true if all students are required to take a math class. D, "Sharon is currently taking a math class" is possibly, but not necessarily, true. She must take a math class at some point while she is a student, but we do not know that she is taking one now.

14. C: 19. First, count the letters of the alphabet to see what number represents each letter. E is the fifth letter of the alphabet, and G is the seventh. There are two Gs and one E in "egg," so, doing the math, we get (2 × 7) + 5 = 19.

15. D: December. The fewest hours of daylight occur at the start of winter, which is mid-December in the Northern Hemisphere. January, July, and October all have more hours of daylight.

16. C: not certain. We know that Mike must submit a time sheet weekly, since he is an employee, but we do not know that he has submitted this week's time sheet yet. It is possible, but not necessarily true, that he has done so already.

17. D: 4,000. First, find out how much the man would pay for 2,000 widgets. 2,000 × 0.50 = $1,000. He has paid more than that, so put that 2,000 figure aside and figure out how many more widgets he has bought than 2,000. He has paid $500 more at the lower rate. Dividing $500 by 0.25 gets us 2,000. Add back in the original 2,000 widgets he bought at the higher rate, and we see that he has bought 4,000 widgets in total.

18. A: have similar meanings. Both words are nearly synonymous, meaning to bewilder someone or misidentify two things as being the same.

19. D: All three of the other shapes have exactly five sides, while D has four sides. Other factors to consider might be whether the sides are all the same length, and whether all the angles are convex, or outward facing, but in both cases, there is more than one figure that breaks that pattern. The number of sides is the only characteristic where exactly one figure breaks the pattern.

20. C: both offer equal value. To compare these figures, simply divide the miles by the dollars to get the mile-per-dollar value. 50,000 ÷ $500 = 100, and 40,000 ÷ $400 = 100. Both offer a rate of 100 miles per dollar, so they are of equal value.

21. Answer: Revert. Revive, resume, and renew all use the "re-" prefix in the sense of repeating or doing something again. To "revive" is to bring to life again or to become alive again, to "resume" is to assume again or take up again, and to "renew" is to make new again.

To "revert," however, uses the re- prefix in the sense of backward movement; i.e., going back to a previous state.

22. Answer: 0.003. To find the answer, reformat all numbers so they can be more easily compared. Since the list contains two fractions, change them to decimals, and extend all numbers to three decimal places. Reformatting our list, we get

0.333   3.000   0.300   0.030   0.003

Now it is easy to see that 0.003 is the smallest number in the list.

23. C: not certain. Joe and Sally know one another, and Sally knows Ian, but it does not follow that Joe and Ian must know one another. They may, or they may not, but their relationship with Sally does not determine whether they know one another or not.

24. B: 40 miles an hour. If the second person takes three hours to drive to a city 120 miles away, dividing 120 by 3 gets us 40 miles per hour.

25. A: obey. While it is possible that the man could fail to see the sign about dangerous weather conditions, the fact that the judge cites him for reckless driving suggests that he did see the sign but chose not to follow it.

26. C: disillusionment. "abracadabra" contains five unique letters, "onomatopoeia" contains eight, and "disillusionment" contains ten.

27. B: 10. This question is solved in two steps. First, we figure out how old the man's sister is. If he is 30, and he is 1.5 times as old as she is now, dividing 30 by 1.5 gets us 20. If she is 20 and he is 30, when she was born (i.e., when she was 0 years old), he was 10, which we get by subtracting her current age from his current age.

28. Regret. All three other verbs can refer to creating an effect on someone else, whereas regret is an internal emotion.

29. C: In the other three figures, all sides are the same length, but in figure C, the bottom side is shorter than the other two sides. Other things to consider might be the number of sides in each figure, but since two figures have three sides, we can dismiss that idea.

30. B: $85. First, figure out what buying 10 plants will cost the customer. At $6 each, 10 plants will cost $60, because 10 × 6 = 60. Subtract 10 from 15 to see how many plants they are buying at the lower rate, and we get 5. If the lower rate is $5, and the customer buys 5, they spend an additional $25. $25 + $60 = $85.

Practice Test #2

Practice Questions

1. An elevator leaves the first floor of a 25-story building with 3 people on board. It stops at every floor. Each time it comes to an even-numbered floor, 3 people get on and one person gets off. Each time it comes to an odd-numbered floor, 3 people get on and 4 people get off. How many people are on board when it arrives at the 25th floor?
   a. 13
   b. 16
   c. 15
   d. 12

2. Which word does not belong with the others?
   a. Artificial
   b. Synthetic
   c. Natural
   d. Man-made

3. The bowl of change on your dresser totals $2.17. Which combination of coins could NOT be in the bowl?
   a. 8 quarters, 1 dime, 1 nickel, and 2 pennies
   b. 192 pennies and 1 quarter
   c. 25 nickels, 11 dimes, and 2 pennies
   d. 6 quarters, 6 dimes, 1 nickel, and 2 pennies

4. *Choose the meaning of the underlined word.*
The group hiked along a <u>precipitous</u> slope that many found unnerving.
   a. rugged
   b. dangerous
   c. steep
   d. wet

5. If 12 is added to the product of 13 and 7, the result is
   a. 32
   b. 79
   c. 103
   d. 240

6. Bernie arrived late for the performance. Tom arrived before Darius. Tom arrived after Bernie. If the first two statements are true, then the third is:
    a. True
    b. False
    c. Unknown

7. What number is one half the average of 3, 4, and 5?
    a. 1.5
    b. 2
    c. 4
    d. 2.5

8. What is the mode of the following numbers: 14, 17, 14, 12, 13, 15, 22, 11?
    a. 13.5
    b. 14
    c. 14.75
    d. 16.5

9. A music download takes 15 minutes for the first 20%. If it continues at the same rate, what will be the total amount of time required to download the entire piece of music?
    a. 1 hour 15 minutes
    b. 1 hour
    c. 50 minutes
    d. 45 minutes

10. Multiplying a number by $\frac{2}{3}$ is the same as dividing that same number by
    a. $\frac{2}{3}$
    b. $\frac{2}{3}$
    c. 1
    d. 3/2

11. *Choose the meaning of the underlined word.*
Stanley was so <u>besotted</u> with his prom date that he spent most of the dance gazing at her adoringly.
    a. infatuated
    b. infuriated
    c. perplexed
    d. engrossed

12. What number added to 23 makes a number equal to one half of 94?
   a. 21
   b. 23
   c. 24
   d. 26

13. On his last math test, Sam got 2 questions correct for every 3 questions he missed. If the test had a total of 60 questions, how many questions did Sam answer correctly?
   a. 12
   b. 24
   c. 36
   d. 60

14. What two numbers should come next in the series 1, 1, 2, 3, 5, 8, 13, ...?
   a. 18, 24
   b. 20, 28
   c. 21, 29
   d. 21, 34

15. Ellie was born one minute after Dean. Dean was born before Rob. Rob was born after Ellie. If the first two statements are true, then the third is:
   a. True
   b. False
   c. Unknown

16. Put the following integers in order from greatest to least:
   -52, 16, -12, 14, 8, -5, 0
   a. -52, 16, -12, 14, 8, -5, 0
   b. 0, -5, 8, -12, 14, 16, -52
   c. 0, -5, -12, -52, 8, 14, 16
   d. -52, -12, -5, 0, 8, 14, 16

17. Which of the following figures has rotational symmetry?

   a.

   b. B)

   c. C)

   d. D)

18. If an odd number is added to an even number, the result must be
    a. odd
    b. even
    c. positive
    d. zero

19. If number x is subtracted from 27, the result is -5. What is number x?
    a. 22
    b. 25
    c. 32
    d. 35

20. The ratio of blue food coloring to yellow food coloring used in making green cake frosting is 3 to 2. If 18 drops of blue food coloring are used, how many drops of yellow food coloring are needed?
    a. 2
    b. 6
    c. 8
    d. 12

21. What geometric figure is this?

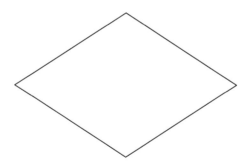

    a. rhombus
    b. trapezoid
    c. pentagon
    d. square

22. A combination lock uses a 3-digit code. Each digit can be any one of the ten available integers 0-9. How many different combinations are possible?
    a. 9
    b. 1,000
    c. 81
    d. 100

23. During the month of November, the Jones family spent $106.20 on fuel costs for their home. What was the average cost per day?
    a. $3.43
    b. $3.54
    c. $5.31
    d. $15.17

24. Richard buys two cups of coffee every day except Saturday and Sunday. On Saturday he buys only one cup, and on Sunday he buys none. If a cup of coffee costs $2.25, how much does Richard spend on coffee every week?
    a. $25.00
    b. $23.50
    c. $24.75
    d. $25.25

25. A shipping clerk can process 180 orders per hour. He has an assistant who can process 180 orders in 90 minutes. How many minutes will it take the two of them, working together, to process 115 orders?
    a. 36
    b. 23
    c. 27
    d. 30

26. Mackenzie left the daycare right after Austin. Nora left right before Austin. Mackenzie left before Austin. If the first two statements are true, then the third is:
    a. True
    b. False
    c. Unknown

27. *Choose the meaning of the underlined word.*
Saline is taking a philosophy class but finds most of the readings to be very obscure, so she has not benefited much from them.
    a. opinionated
    b. unclear
    c. offensive
    d. benign

28. Which number could fill in the blank in this sequence? 1, 6, 16, __, 51
    a. 31
    b. 26
    c. 41
    d. 21

29. Which word does not belong with the others?
    a. Painter
    b. Artist
    c. Musician
    d. Dancer

30. Shun means the *opposite* of
    a. Return
    b. Embrace
    c. Manipulate
    d. Retract

Answers and Explanations

1. B: There are 12 even-numbered floors between floors 1 and 25. At each one, the elevator gains 2 people, for a net gain of 24. There are 11 odd-numbered floors between floors 1 and 25 (not counting floors 1 and 25). At each one, the elevator loses 1 person, for a net loss of 11. The elevator leaves the first floor with 3 people, so the total arriving at the 25th floor is 3 + 24 – 11 = 16.

2. C: Natural is the opposite of the other words in the series. Artificial, synthetic, and man-made are all words for non-natural processes.

3. C: This combination of coins totals $2.37.

4. C: The word "precipitous" means "steep."

5. C: The product is the result of multiplying two numbers.
The product of 13 x 7 = 91. Add 12 to get 103, Choice C.

6. C: We can diagram this sentence as follows: Tom > Darius, which tells us that Tom arrived before Darius. We do not have enough information to determine when Bernie arrived in relation to the other two people.

7. B: To compute the average, first find the sum of all the items in the list and then divide by the number of items in the list. This yields $\dfrac{3+4+5}{3} = \dfrac{12}{3} = 4$. One half of 4 is 2.

8. B: The mode is the value of the term that occurs most. Of these terms, the number 14 occurs twice, so Choice B is the correct answer.

9. A: Since 20% is equivalent to 1/5, it will take 5 times as long to download the entire piece of music. 5 x 15 = 75 minutes, this is equivalent to 1 hour 15 minutes.

10. D: Division is the opposite, or the reciprocal, of multiplication.
The reciprocal of ⅔ is $^3/_2$, Choice D.

11. A: Besotted means infatuated.

12. C: One half of 94 equals 47. Since 47 – 23 = 24, C is the correct answer.

13. B: The ratio of correct to incorrect answers is 2:3, giving a whole of 5. It takes 12 sets of 5 questions to total 60 questions. To determine how many correct answers Sam gave, multiply 2 by 12, for a total of 24, Choice B.

14. D: In this series, each number is the sum of the two preceding numbers. For example, 3 = 1 + 2, and 5 = 3 + 2. Therefore, the number following 13 must be 13 + 8 = 21, and the next number must be 21 + 13 = 34.

15. C: We can diagram this sentence as follows: Dean > Ellie; Dean > Rob. In other words, Dean was born before Ellie and before Rob. We do not have enough information to determine whether Ellie > Rob is true.

16. D: Think of the numbers as they would be on a number line to place them in the correct order.

17. D: Rotational symmetry is defined as a figure that looks exactly the same after being rotated any amount. Answer choice D is the only example given that would stay the same if rotated.

18. A: An odd number can be considered as an even number N plus 1. Two even numbers added together produce an even number, so the result of adding an odd and an even number must be an even number plus 1, which is odd. For example, 4 + 3 = 7.

19. C: In this problem, if you do not know how to solve, try filling in the answer choices to see which one checks out. Many math problems may be solved by a guess and check method when you have a selection of answer choices.
$27 - x = -5$
$x = 32$

20. D: Set up and solve a proportion. To solve the proportion, cross-multiply:
$\frac{3}{18} = \frac{2}{x}$
$3x = 36$
$x = 12$, Choice D.

21. A
A rhombus is four-sided polygon having all four sides of equal length. The sum of the angles of a rhombus is 360 degrees.

22. B: In this probability problem there are three independent events (the codes for each digit), each with ten possible outcomes (the numerals 0-9). Since the events are independent, the total possible outcomes equals the product of the possible outcomes for each of the three events, that is $P = P_1 \times P_2 \times P_3 = 10 \times 10 \times 10 = 1,000$

23. B: The average cost for the month is calculated by dividing the total cost ($106.20) by 30 (the number of days in November).

24. C: Since he buys two cups per day for five days, and one cup on Saturday, the total number of cups that Richard buys each week is (2 x 5) + 1 = 11 cups. Since each cup costs $2.25, the amount he spends is 11 x $2.25 = $24.75.

25. B: At 180 orders per hour, the clerk processes 3 orders per minute, since there are 60 minutes in an hour ($\frac{180}{60} = 3$). His assistant processes 2 orders per minute ($\frac{180}{90} = 2$).

Together, they can process 3 + 2 = 5 orders per minute. Therefore, 115 orders will take $\frac{115}{5} = 23$ minutes.

26. B: We can diagram the first two sentences as follows: Mackenzie > Austin; Nora > Austin. The third sentence, which we could diagram as Mackenzie < Austin, contradicts the first sentence.

27. B: The word "obscure" means "unclear" and "difficult to understand."

28. A: The sequence increases by multiples of 5: to get from 1 to 6, add 5. To get from 6 to 16, add 10. To get from 16 to 31, add 15. To get from 31 to 51, add 20.

29. B: "Artist" is the general category that all the other items in the series belong to; painters, musicians, and dancers are all kinds of artists.

30. B: Shun means reject or ignore, the opposite of embrace.

Practice Test #3

Practice Questions

1. The gardeners planted the sapling several yards from the other trees in order to **accommodate** the tree's future growth.

In this context, **accommodate** most nearly means:
   a. Host
   b. Allow
   c. Restrict

2. Look at the row of numbers below.

    27   9   3   1   ?

What number should come next?
   a. 0
   b. 3
   c. 1/3
   d. 1/9

3. Assume the following two statements are true:
   > All children must be vaccinated before being allowed to attend school.
   > Miguel does not attend school.

Which of the following statements could be logically concluded?
   a. Miguel has been vaccinated
   b. Miguel has not been vaccinated
   c. Miguel is not allowed to attend school
   d. None of these can be logically concluded

4. A certain recipe for a dozen cookies requires 3/4 of a cup of flour. To triple the recipe, how much flour would a cook require?
   a. 2 1/4 cups
   b. 2 1/2 cups
   c. 2 3/4 cups
   d. 3 cups

5. The seventh month of the year is:
   a. July
   b. August
   c. September
   d. October

6. Observe the following shape:

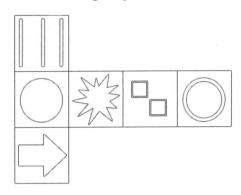

If this shape were folded into a cube, which of the following could result?

a.

b.

c.

d.

7. What percentage is equal to 0.75?
  a. 75%
  b. 750%
  c. 7.5%
  d. 0.75%

8. The manager made efforts to **temper** her criticism with praise so the employee would not feel upset.

In this context, **temper** most nearly means
  a. Anger
  b. Combine
  c. Soften

9. Look at the row of numbers below.

4   8   24   96   ?

What number should come next?
  a. 72
  b. 120
  c. 384
  d. 480

10. A man is packing for a trip. If he packs three shirts, four pairs of pants, and two pairs of socks, how many days can he go without repeating any item of clothing?
  a. 2 days
  b. 3 days
  c. 9 days
  d. 24 days

41. Which word does not fit in the following list?
        sketch   portfolio   blueprint   painting

12. Three of the four figures below are identical, but rotated. Which one is different?

a.

b.

c.

d.

13. Assume the first two statements are true.
        1. All soccer team members bring their own ball to practice.
        2. Jana is a soccer team member.
        3. Jana brings her own ball to practice.

The third statement is:
  a. True
  b. False
  c. Not certain

14. A woman is on vacation for three days and wants to go to a museum, the beach, and the mountains. Assuming she does each activity only once, in how many different orders can she do them?

    a. 3
    b. 5
    c. 6
    d. 27

15. If the last day of February is a Sunday, what day will the 28th of March fall on?

    a. Sunday
    b. Wednesday
    c. Friday
    d. Saturday

16. How many of the five pairs of items listed below are exact duplicates?

Bob Roberts	Rob Roberts
Shawn Phillips	Shaun Phillips
T.J. Paine	T.J. Paine
Tom Jensen	Tom Jansen
Pete Jacobs	Pete Jacobs

17. A student averaged 80 points on five tests. The first four scores were 78, 74, 82, and 86. What was the score on the last test?

    a. 70
    b. 75
    c. 80
    d. 82

18.   AUGMENT   SUPPLEMENT

These words have:

    a. Similar meanings
    b. Contradictory meanings
    c. Neither similar nor contradictory meanings

19. Look at the row of numbers below. What number should come next?

    1   2   0   1   −1   0   ?

    a. – 2
    b. – 1
    c. 0
    d. 1

20. It was sunny for ten days in January. January has 31 days. Approximately what percentage of the total days in January was it sunny?
    a. 1%
    b. 3%
    c. 10%
    d. 30%

21. Each week, Zach visits his local ice cream shop and orders one of the four flavors randomly. After how many weeks can he ensure having tasted all four flavors?
    a. 4
    b. 5
    c. 8
    d. Cannot be determined

22. Which word does not belong with the others?
    a. Toaster
    b. Oven
    c. Appliance
    d. Coffee maker

23. Samuel invented more patents than his brother James. Horace had twice as many patents as James. Samuel and Horace had the same number of patents. If the first two statements are true, then the third is:
    a. True
    b. False
    c. Unknown

24. On Frank's bus ride to work, all available seats are filled and 6 passengers are standing in the aisles. If 10 passengers get off the bus and 8 others get on, how many passengers are standing in the aisles, assuming that all available seats continue to be filled?
    a. 2
    b. 4
    c. 6
    d. 8

25. The sum of two negative numbers
    a. is always negative.
    b. is always positive.
    c. sometimes is positive and sometimes is negative/
    d. is always zero.

26. All of the children are girls. Some of the girls like soccer. Some of the girls like cheerleading. Based on this data, which statement has to be correct?
    a. All girls like to play soccer.
    b. Some of the girls are 3 years old.
    c. Some of the girls like both soccer and cheerleading.
    d. Some of the children like soccer.

27. What is the next number in the series?
        132, 123, 115, 108, 102
    a. 82
    b. 87
    c. 92
    d. 97

28. Otis caught more beads than Steve at Mardi Gras. Steve got as many beads as Carrie. Carrie got fewer beads than Otis. If the first two statements are true, then the third is:
    a. True
    b. False
    c. Unknown

29. Which of the following is the largest number?
    a. 1/2
    b. 3/8
    c. 7/16
    d. 13/54

30. Esther drove the same distance as Marcus. Lee drove twice as far as Marcus. Esther drove farther than Lee. If the first two statements are true, then the third is:
    a. True
    b. False
    c. Unknown

Answers and Explanations

1. B: allow. While "host" is a common meaning of "accommodate," here the gardeners are allowing room for the tree to grow larger in the future.

2. C: 1/3. Each number is found by dividing the previous one by 3. 27 ÷ 3 = 9, and 9 ÷ 3 = 3, and 3 ÷ 3 = 1. 1 ÷ 3 = 1/3, so that is the next number in the series.

3. D: none of these can be logically concluded. We don't know that the reason Miguel doesn't attend school is because he hasn't been vaccinated. He might be an infant, or an adult, for example.

4. A: 2 1/4 cups. To triple the recipe, multiply the numerator (3) by 3, getting 9/4. 4 goes into 9 twice, with 1 left over, so our end result is 2 1/4 cups.

5. A: July. Simply count the months of the year. January, February, March, April, May, June, and July represent seven months.

6. A: This is the only figure in which the three faces shown could appear in that orientation on a cube made from the two-dimensional shape given. In choice B, the two circles could be next to the other two figures, but the three stripes should be facing the other way. In choice C, the two squares should be on the side of the cube we cannot see, if we see the other two figures. In choice D, the arrow and the stripes could not be visible at the same time; they should be on opposite sides of the cube. Choice A is the only one that is logically possible.

7. A: 75%. 0.75 means seventy-five one-hundredths, or 75 parts per hundred. Percent means the same thing: parts per hundred. So 75% is the equivalent to 0.75.

8. C: soften. While "temper" sometimes refers to a person's quickness to anger, here it means to soften. While she is combining the criticism and praise, she is doing so in a specific way that is better described by "soften."

9. D: 480. The series of numbers is formed by multiplying the previous number by increasing factors: 4 × 2 = 8, then 8 × 3 = 24, then 24 × 4 = 96. So the next operation is to multiply 96 by 5, resulting in 480.

10. A: 2 days. This question actually doesn't require any math! To find out how long he can go without repeating any items of clothing, simply look at the category of clothing that has the smallest number of items in it. In this case, it is socks; the man has two pairs of socks. On day three, he'll have to repeat a pair of socks. So the answer is two days with no repeats.

11. B: The other three items in the list are single units, while a portfolio is a collection of items such as these.

12. B: In all three other answer choices, the line stretches across its section of the square, but in choice B, it points into the corner.

13. A: Answer: A, true. If all soccer team members bring their own ball to practice, and Jana is a soccer team member, then she must bring her own ball to practice.

14. C: 6. To find the answer, simply multiply together the woman's available activity choices on each day. On day one, she can do any of the three activities. On day two, she can do either of the remaining two activities, and on day three, she can do the one remaining activity. Multiplying these together, we get 3 × 2 × 1 = 6.

15. A: Sunday. If the last day of February is a Sunday, then the 28th of March falls 28 days later. (This is true whether February has 28 or 29 days in it in a given year.) Because 28 is a multiple of 7, the 28th of March will fall exactly 4 weeks later, on the same day as the last day of February.

16. Two are exact duplicates, T.J. Paine and Pete Jacobs. In the first pair, Bob and Rob do not match. In the second, Shawn and Shaun are spelled differently. In the fourth pair, Jensen and Jansen are spelled differently.

17. C: 80. To find the missing score, work backward. Multiply the average of 80 by the number of tests (in this case, five), then subtract out all the known scores to find the missing score. 80 × 5 = 400, and 400 – 78 –74 – 82 – 86 = 80.

18. A: Answer: A, have similar meanings. Both words refer to increasing the amount of something. "To augment" is to make bigger, while "to supplement" is to add to something.

19. A: –2. There is a two-step pattern going on here. First, we add 1, then we subtract 2. 1 + 1 = 2, then 2 – 2 = 0. 0 + 1 = 1, then 1 – 2 = –1. –1 + 1 = 0, so the next thing to do is subtract 2, giving us –2.

20. D: 30%. Ten out of 31 days is roughly 1/3, or about 30%.

21. D: Just as flipping a coin any number of times could result in the same outcome (heads or tails) each time, ordering randomly (if such a thing is possible) is no guarantee that all flavors will eventually be ordered. This is different from problems in which people select a jelly bean out of a pot and remove it from consideration for the next selection; because jelly beans are removed from consideration, that scenario ensures that all jelly beans will eventually be chosen.

22. C: "Appliance" is a general category that the other words in the list belong to. Toasters, ovens, and coffee makers are all appliances.

23. C: We can diagram the first two sentences as follows: Samuel > James; Horace > James. These sentences do not give us enough information to prove sentence three, Samuel = Horace.

24. B: After the 10 passengers get off the bus, presumably no one will be standing in the aisles and there will be 4 vacant seats. After the 8 new passengers board, 4 of them will fill the vacant seats and the other 4 will be left to stand in the aisles. It is also possible to calculate the answer by assigning any number to the number of seats on the bus. For instance, if there are 20 seats on the bus, then at the start of the problem there are 26

passengers. After 10 get off, there are 16 passengers, and after 8 get on, there are then 24 passengers. The first 20 passengers would fill the available seats, and the other 4 would stand in the aisles.

25. A: Negative numbers represent segments extending to the left of zero on the number line. Adding a negative number to another negative number extends the segment even further to the left, or into "negative territory". To add two negative numbers, add the magnitudes and retain the negative sign. For example
$(-3) + (-5) = -8$.

26. D: If all of the children are girls, and some of the girls like soccer, then some of the children must like soccer. None of the other statements can be deduced from the information given.

27. D: The pattern is subtracting one less number each time:
$$132 - 9 = 123$$
$$123 - 8 = 115$$
$$115 - 7 = 108$$
$$108 - 6 = 102$$
The next number to be subtracted is 5, so $102 - 5 = 97$

28. A: We can diagram the first two sentences as follows: Otis > Steve = Carrie. The third sentence claims that Otis > Carrie, which is consistent with the first two sentences.

29. A: The fraction of ½ is the same as 50%. None of the other fractions are equal to that.

30. B: The first two sentences can be diagrammed as follows: Esther = Marcus; Lee > Marcus. If Lee drove farther than Marcus, he also drove farther than Esther. The third sentence, which we can diagram as Esther > Lee, contradicts sentences one and two, so it is false.

Wonderlic Skill Building Questions

Mathematics Practice 1 Questions

1. 25% of 400 =
    a. 100
    b. 200
    c. 800
    d. 10,000

2. 22% of $900 =
    a. 90
    b. 198
    c. 250
    d. 325

3. Which of these numbers is a factor of 21?
    a. 2
    b. 5
    c. 7
    d. 42

4. (9÷3) x (8÷4) =
    a. 1
    b. 6
    c. 72
    d. 576

5. Once inch equals 2.54 cm. How many centimeters tall is a 76- inch man.
    a. 20 cm
    b. 29.92 cm
    c. 193.04 cm
    d. 300.04 cm

6. What is the reciprocal of 6?
    a. ½
    b. 1/3
    c. 1/6
    d. 1/12

7. A room measures 11 ft x 12 ft x 9 ft. What is the volume?
    a. 1188 ft³
    b. 32 ft³
    c. 120 ft³
    d. 1300 ft³

8. A roast was cooked at 325 °F in the oven for 4 hours. The internal temperature rose from 32 °F to 145 °F. What was the average rise in temperature per hour?
    a. 20.2 °F/hr
    b. 28.25°F/hr
    c. 32.03°F/hr
    d. 37°F/hr

9. You need to purchase a textbook for school. The book cost $80.00, and the sales tax where you are purchasing the book is 8.25%. You have $100. How much change will you receive back?
    a. $5.20
    b. $7.35
    c. $13.40
    d. $19.95

10. You purchase a car making a down payment of $3,000 and 6 monthly payments of $225. How much have you paid so far for the car?
    a. $3225
    b. $4350
    c. $5375
    d. $6550

11. Your supervisor instructs you to purchase 240 pens and 6 staplers for the nurse's station. Pens are purchase in sets of 6 for $2.35 per pack. Staplers are sold in sets of 2 for 12.95. How much will purchasing these products cost?
    a. $132.85
    b. $145.75
    c. $162.90
    d. $225.05

12. Which of the following percentages is equal to 0.45?
    a. 0.045%
    b. 0.45%
    c. 4.5%
    d. 45%

13. A vitamin's expiration date has passed. It was suppose to contain 500 mg of Calcium, but it has lost 325 mg of Calcium. How many mg of Calcium is left?
    a. 135 mg
    b. 175 mg
    c. 185 mg
    d. 200 mg

14. You have orders to give a patient 20 mg of a certain medication. The medication is stored 4 mg per 5-mL dose. How many milliliters will need to be given?
    a. 15 mL
    b. 20 mL
    c. 25 mL
    d. 30 mL

15. In the number 743.25 which digit represents the tenths space?
    a. 2
    b. 3
    c. 4
    d. 5

16. Which of these percentages equals 1.25?
    a. 0.125%
    b. 12.5%
    c. 125%
    d. 1250%

17. If the average person drinks 8, (8oz) glasses of water per day, a person who drinks 12.8 oz of water after a morning exercise session has consumed what fraction of the daily average?
    a. 1/3
    b. 1/5
    c. 1/7
    d. 1/9

18. If y = 3, then $y^3(y^3-y)=$
    a. 300
    b. 459
    c. 648
    d. 999

19. 33% of 300 =
    a. 3
    b. 9
    c. 33
    d. 99

20. You need 4/5 cups of water for a recipe. You accidentally put 1/3 cups into the mixing bowl with the dry ingredients. How much more water in cups do you need to add?
    a. 1/3 cups
    b. 2/3 cups
    c. 1/15 cups
    d. 7/15 cups

21. ¾ - ½ =
   a. ¼
   b. 1/3
   c. ½
   d. 2/3

22. You cannot find your 1 cup measuring cup. You can only locate your ¼ measuring cup. Your recipe calls for 2 ½ cups of flour. How many times will you need to fill your ¼ measuring cup with flour for the recipe?
   a. 4
   b. 6
   c. 8
   d. 10

23. You are financing a computer for $5000. You are required to put down a 15% down payment. How much money do you need for your down payment?
   a. $500
   b. $650
   c. $750
   d. $900

24. You are traveling in Europe, and you see a sign stating that London is 3 kilometers away. If 1 kilometer is equal to 0.625 miles, how many miles away is London from where you are?
   a. 0.208 miles
   b. 1.875 miles
   c. 2.75 miles
   d. 3 miles

25. You need exactly a 1680 ft3 aquarium for your fish. At the pet store you see four choices of aquariums, but the volume is not listed. The length, width, and height are listed on the box. Which of the following aquariums would fit your needs?
   a. 12 ft x 12 ft x 12 ft
   b. 13 ft x 15 ft x 16 ft
   c. 14 ft x 20 ft x 6 ft
   d. 15 ft x 16 ft x 12 ft

26. You invested $9,000 and received yearly interest of $450. What is your interest rate on your investment?
   a. 5%
   b. 6%
   c. 7%
   d. 8%

27. In your class there are 48 students, 32 students are female. Approximately what percentage is male?
    a. 25%
    b. 33%
    c. 45%
    d. 66%

28. If w = 82 +2, and z = 41 (2), then
    a. w<z
    b. w>z
    c. w-z = 1
    d. w=z

29. After talking with his girlfriend on the telephone long distance, a student calculates the amount of money he spent on the call. The first 20 minutes were 99 cents, and each additional minute was 10 cents. He calculated that his phone call cost $ 5.49. How long was his call?
    a. 40 minutes
    b. 45 minutes
    c. 65 minutes
    d. 75 minutes

30. You are teaching a community education class on fire safety to children. There are 6 first graders, 7 second graders, and 5 third graders. What percentage of the class are second graders?
    a. 28%
    b. 33%
    c. 39%
    d. 48%

31. One slice of bread is 80 calorie. Approximately how many calories are in 2 ½ slices of bread?
    a. 140 calories
    b. 200 calories
    c. 220 calories
    d. 240 calories

32. 7x = 3a + 2a. If a = 7, then x =
    a. 5
    b. 7
    c. 9
    d. 12

Use the following formula for answering Question 33:
Fried's rule for computing an infant's dose of medication is:

infant's dose = Child's age in months X adult dose
150

33. If the adult dose of medication is 15 mg, how much should be given to a 2 year-old child?
   a. 1.2
   b. 2.4
   c. 3.6
   d. 4.8

34. What is the area of a triangle if the base is 6 cm and the height is 8 cm.
   a. 18 cm²
   b. 20 cm²
   c. 22 cm²
   d. 24 cm²

35. 7 ½ - 5 3/8 =
   a. 1 1/2
   b. 1 2/3
   c. 2 1/8
   d. 3 1/4

36. The school's softball team won 15 games, but lost 10. What was ratio of wins to losses?
   a. 2:1
   b. 3:1
   c. 3:2
   d. 4:1

37. 35 is 20% of what number?
   a. 175
   b. 186
   c. 190
   d. 220

38. 6 x 0 x 5
   a. 30
   b. 11
   c. 25
   d. 0

39. 7.95 ÷ 1.5
   a. 2.4
   b. 5.3
   c. .2
   d. 7.3

40. If x = 4, then 2x + 7x =
    a. 24
    b. 27
    c. 35
    d. 36

41. 7/10 equals:
    a. 0.007
    b. 0.07
    c. 0.7
    d. 1.7

42. 4/8 equals:
    a. 0.005
    b. 0.05
    c. 0.5
    d. 5

43. 8/24 equals:
    a. 1/6
    b. 1/4
    c. 1/8
    d. 1/3

44. 83,000 equals:
    a. 83.0×10^5
    b. 8.3×10^4
    c. 8.3×10^{-4}
    d. 83.0×10^{-3}

45. .00875 equals:
    a. 8.75×10^1
    b. 8.75×10^{-3}
    c. 8.75×10^3
    d. 87.5×10^4

46. –32 + 7 equals:
    a. –25
    b. 25
    c. –26
    d. 26

47. –37 + -47 equals:
    a. 84
    b. –84
    c. 10
    d. –10

48. 41% equals:
    a. 4.1
    b. 0.41
    c. 0.041
    d. 0.0041

49. 22(5x) =
    a. 110x
    b. 4.4 x
    c. 110x^2
    d. 4.4 x^2

Answer Key for Mathematics Practice 1

1. A: (400 x .25) = 100

2. B: ($900 x .22) = 198

3. C: (Factors are numbers that can divide evenly into a certain number. 7 can divide into 21 three times.)

4. B: (3) x (2) = 6

5. C: 1/2.54 = 76/x; x = 2.54 (76), x= 193.04

6. C: The reciprocal of a fraction is the inverse of the fraction. The fraction is turned upside down. 6 = 6/1, the reciprocal is 1/6.

7. A: 11 ft x 12ft x 19 ft = 1188 ft³

8. B: 145°F-32°F = 113°F, 113°F ÷4hrs = 28.25°F/ hr

9. C: $80 x 0.825= $6.60, $ 80+ $6.60= $86.60, $100-$86.60= $13.40

10. B: $3000 + ($225(6 payments)= $4350

11. A: 240÷6 = 40, 6÷2=3, (40 packs of pens x $2.35 ea.) + (3 packs of staplers x $12.95 ea.) =$132.85

12. D: .45 x 100 = 45%

13. B: 500mg Ca – 325 mg Ca = 175 mg Ca

14. C: set up ration of 4/5 = 20/x, 4x= 20(5), x = 100/4, x= 25 mL dose

15. A: moving right of the decimal point one space is the tenths position

16. C: 1.25 x 100= 125%

17. B: 12.8 ÷ 64 = .20. .20= 20/100, reduce 20/100 to 1/5

18. C: 27(27-3)= 27(24) = 648

19. D: 300 x .33= 99

20. D: 4/5 –1/3, find common denominator, 12/15-5/15= 7/15 cups

21. A: ¾ - ½ = ¾ - 2/4 = ¼

22. D: 2 ½ converts to 5/2, find common denominator 10/4 ÷ ¼ = 10 cups

23. C: $5000 x .15 = $750

24. B: .625 x 3 = 1.875 miles, you can also set up as a ratio

25. C: 14 ft x 20 ft x 6 ft = 1680 ft³

26. A: 450 ÷ 9000 = .05, .05 x 100= 5%

27. B: 48 students – 32 girls = 16 boys, 16 ÷ 48= .33, .33 x 100=33%

28. B: w=84, y = 82, 84>82

29. C: .99 + .10 (x) = $5.49, .10 x= 5.49-.99, x= 4.50/.10, x= 45, 45+20=65 mins (Don't forget the original 20 minutes from the flat rate of 99 cents.)

30. C: 7÷18= .38, .38 x 100 = 38%

31. B: 80 calories x 2.5 slices of bread = 200 calories

32. A: 7x= 21+14, 35 ÷ 7 = x, x=5

33. B: infant dose = (24 months ÷ 150) 15 mg= 2.4mg

34. D: ½ (b) (h) = ½ (6) (8)= 24 cm³

35. C: (15/2) – (43/8)= (60/8)- (43/8)= 17/8 = 2 1/8

36. C: 3:2 both 15 and 10 are divisible by 5

37. A: 20% is 1/5 of a number 1/5 = 35/x. 1x= 35(5), x = 175

38. D: any number multiplied by 0 is equal to 0

39. B: 7.95 ÷1.5= 5.3, remember to move decimal point one place over before beginning equation

40. D: 2(4) + 7(4) = 8 + 28= 36

41. C: 7 Divided by 10 = .7

42. C: 4/8 reduced to ½, 1 divided by 2 = .5

43. D: 8 goes into 8 = 1, 8 goes into 24, = 3

44. B: If the decimal moves to the left the ⁴ is positive.

45. B: If the decimal moves to the right the $^{-3}$ is negative.

46. A: –25, Add the positive and negative numbers together.

47. B: Add the two negative numbers together

48. B: 41 Divided by 100 equals .41

49. A: 110x There are no exponents to multiply together.

Verbal Practice 1

Pick the word that is most appropriate.

1. John prefers _____ art to the classics.
    a. Contemporary
    b. Contemperary
    c. Contemparary
    d. Conteporary

2. Allen told Steve that he would give him the ____ version of his morning when he had time.
    a. Unabridgged
    b. Unabriddged
    c. Unabbridged
    d. Unabridged

3. Lisa was known for having _____ relationships.
    a. Promiscous
    b. Promicuous
    c. Promiscuous
    d. Promicious

4. The new tax was passed for _____ the waterfront district.
    a. Revitallizing
    b. Revitalizzing
    c. Revitelizing
    d. Revitalizing

5. The increased _____ to the class fund allowed for an end of the year party.
    a. Revenuee
    b. Revenue
    c. Revanue
    d. Revanuee

6. The teenager _____ some candy from the grocery store.
    a. Pillferred
    b. Pilferred
    c. Pillfered
    d. Pilfered

7. Being from a small town, some of Dean's views were _____.
    a. Parochial
    b. Perochial
    c. Porochial
    d. Parochiel

8. All of the students dreaded the quizzes the professor gave since he tested on _____
material.
   a. Obscere
   b. Obscore
   c. Obbscure
   d. Obscure

9. The judge sued the newspaper for ____.
   a. Libel
   b. Labal
   c. Lobel
   d. Libbel

Identify the key word/words that complete the statements 10-20.

10. The _____ of the rainbow were _____ against the bright blue sky.
    a. Textures, Clear
    b. Hues, Vivid
    c. Alabaster, Bright
    d. Line, Dark

11. The president has a _____ of _____ around him when he makes public appearances.
    a. Catalyst, Individuals
    b. Barrier, Contrast
    c. Hedge, Protection
    d. Derrick, Protection

12. A small selection of terms was found at the back of the textbook. It was a
    a. Glossary
    b. Preface
    c. Diction
    d. Kefir

13. The horror movie frightened the children. It was
    a. Melancholy
    b. Dramatic
    c. Ghastly
    d. Tragedy

14. After practice, the girl's softball team stated, "We're famished!"
    Famished means
    a. Fatigued
    b. Hungry
    c. Excited
    d. Ready

15. The newborn baby was enamored with the rattle.
    Enamored means
    a. Fascinated
    b. Happy
    c. Unsure what to do
    d. Aggravated

16. When having a problem, it is best to dissect the situation then act.
    Dissect means
    a. Cut apart
    b. Talk about
    c. Ignore
    d. Analyze

17. The books subject matter was ____ to the ____, and it did not sell.
    a. Attractive, Masses
    b. Limited, People
    c. Loathsome, Masses
    d. Colorful, Individual

18. The kitten was soaked to the ____ from the ___.
    a. Skin, Abyss
    b. Skin, Craven
    c. Skin, Storm
    d. Hide, Abyss

19. The bouncer's countenance discouraged brawls.
    Countenance means
    a. Message
    b. Presence
    c. Expression
    d. Strength

20. The child apprized her father's authority and behaved herself in church.
    Apprized means
    a. Appreciated
    b. Compromised
    c. Defied
    d. Noted

Identify the appropriate error in the following sentences 21-26.

21. David was known for belching; and telling inappropriate jokes in public.
    a. Capitalization
    b. Punctuation
    c. Spelling
    d. Grammar

22. Graduation from High School is considered by many a momentous occasion.
    a. Capitalization
    b. Punctuation
    c. Spelling
    d. Grammar

23. Nurses plays a vital role in the healthcare profession.
    a. Capitalization
    b. Punctuation
    c. Spelling
    d. Grammar

24. After having his tonsels removed, the child was listless for a few days.
    a. Capitalization
    b. Punctuation
    c. Spelling
    d. Grammar

25. The park was serine at twilight.
    a. Capitalization
    b. Punctuation
    c. Spelling
    d. Grammar

26. The patient's mind was lucid during the evaluation?
    a. Capitalization
    b. Punctuation
    c. Spelling
    d. Grammar

Answer Key for Verbal Practice 1

1. A
2. D
3. C
4. D
5. B
6. D
7. A
8. D
9. A
10. B
11. C
12. A
13. C
14. B
15. A
16. D
17. C
18. C
19. C
20. A
21. B
22. A
23. D
24. C
25. C
26. B

Mathematics Practice 2

1. 75% of 500
   a. 365
   b. 375
   c. 387
   d. 390

2. 45% of 600
   a. 250
   b. 260
   c. 270
   d. 280

3. (7 x 5) + (8 x 2) =
   a. 51
   b. 57
   c. 85
   d. 560

4. (8 ÷ 2) (12 ÷ 3) =
   a. 1
   b. 8
   c. 12
   d. 16

5. Which of the following numbers is a prime number?
   a. 12
   b. 25
   c. 27
   d. 31

6. Which number is a factor of 36?
   a. 5
   b. 7
   c. 8
   d. 9

7. 75 x 34 =
   a. 1200
   b. 2050
   c. 2550
   d. 3100

8. x + 372 = 853, x =
   a. 455
   b. 481
   c. 520
   d. 635

9. Convert .25 into fraction form.
   a. ¼
   b. ½
   c. 1/8
   d. 2/3

10. 60 grains are equal to 1 dram. How many grains are in 15 drams?
    a. 900
    b. 1020
    c. 1220
    d. 1300

11. A pitcher holds 7 ½ cups water. How many cups will 5 pitchers hold?
    a. 34 ¼
    b. 35 ½
    c. 37 ½
    d. 38 ¼

12. If a = 3, b= 4, c=5, then $(a + b + c)^2 + (a - b - c) =$
    a. 124
    b. 136
    c. 138
    d. 150

13. 0.85 =
    a. 13/15
    b. 17/20
    c. 18/19
    d. 19/22

14. Which fraction is closest to 2/3 without going over?
    a. 6/13
    b. 7/12
    c. 11/16
    d. 9/12

15. A puddle of water contained 72 pints of water. A rainstorm added 21% more water to the puddle. Approximately, how many pints of water are now in the puddle?
    a. 76
    b. 87
    c. 92
    d. 112

16. If x = 2 then x⁴ (x + 3) =
    a. 72
    b. 80
    c. 96
    d. 114

17. A circle graph is used to show the percent of patient types that a hospital sees. How many degrees of the circle should the graph show if 1/3 of the patient type is pediatric?
    a. 90 degrees
    b. 120 degrees
    c. 220 degrees
    d. 360 degrees

18. A traveler on vacation spent $ 25 at the grocery store the first week of school; the next two weeks he spent $ 52; and the last week he spent $34. What was his average food expenditure while he was on vacation?
    a. $ 37.00
    b. $ 38.25
    c. $ 40.75
    d. $ 52.00

19. 437.65 – 325.752 =
    a. 111.898
    b. 121.758
    c. 122.348
    d. 133.053

20. 43.3 x 23.03 =
    a. 997.199
    b. 999.999
    c. 1010.03
    d. 1111.01

21. How many nonoverlapping 2-inch x 2-inch squares are contained in a 8-inch x 24- inch rectangle?
    a. 32
    b. 44
    c. 48
    d. 52

22. After going on diet for two weeks, you have lost 6% of you weight. Your original weight was 157 lbs. What do you weigh now?
    a. 132 lbs
    b. 135.48 lbs
    c. 144.98 lbs
    d. 147.58 lbs

23. In order for a school to allow a vending machine to be placed next to the cafeteria, 65% of the school's population must ask for it. If 340 of the school's 650 students have requested the vending machines, how many more are needed to get the vending machines?
    a. 75
    b. 83
    c. 89
    d. 99

24. After purchasing a book that has a no return policy, the book goes on sale at the bookstore for 15% less. You realize that you spent an extra $12.75 on the book. What amount did you pay for the book originally?
    a. $65
    b. $75
    c. $85
    d. $95

25. Which of the following fractions have the largest value?
    a. 8/15
    b. 7/12
    c. 6/13
    d. 9/16

26. Round this number to the nearest hundredths 390.24657
    a. 400
    b. 390.247
    c. 390.25
    d. 390.2

27. To get 1 as an answer, you must multiply 4/5 by
    a. 5/4
    b. ½
    c. 1
    d. ¼

28. $z = 4$, $z + 6 - (z+4) =$
    a. 2
    b. 4
    c. 6
    d. 8

29. While working, patient's sodium intake was 300 mg on Monday, 1240 mg on Tuesday, 900 mg on Wednesday and Friday, and 1500 on Thursday. What was the average intake of sodium while the patient was at work?
    a. 476 mg
    b. 754 mg
    c. 968 mg
    d. 998 mg

30. Which of the following numbers is correctly rounded to the nearest tenth?
    a. 3.756 rounds to 3.76
    b. 4.567 rounds to 4.5
    c. 6.982 rounds to 7.0
    d. 54.32 rounds to 54.4

31. 4.2% of 328 =
    a. 12.7
    b. 13.8
    c. 14.2
    d. 15.5

32. Which of the following fraction equal 0.625
    a. 3/4
    b. 5/6
    c. 5/8
    d. 2/3

33. Which of the following illustrates the distributive property of multiplication?
    a. $2x + 5(z - 3) = 10x + 5z - 15$
    b. $2x + 5(z - 3) = 2x + 5z - 3$
    c. $2x + 5(z - 3) = 2x + 5z - 15$
    d. $2x + 5(z - 3) = 2z + z - 15$

34. Which of the following is the square root of 80
    a. $4\sqrt{5}$
    b. 8
    c. $5\sqrt{4}$
    d. 16

Questions 35 to 38 refer to the following information:

A school has a 50 x 60 yard rectangular playground. There are 3 classes playing on it. 15 students are from Mrs. Red's class, 12 are from Miss White's class, and 17 are from Ms. Brown's class.

35. How many square yards does the playground cover?
    a. 110
    b. 300
    c. 3,000
    d. 30,000

36. How many students are playing on the playground?
    a. 15
    b. 22
    c. 36
    d. 44

37. If both sides of the playground are increased by 10%, what would the area be in square yards?
   a. 121
   b. 1210
   c. 3,000
   d. 3,630

38. Ms. Brown's class raised $400 to help put a fence around the playground. The fence cost $15 a yard. How much more money per student would Ms. Brown's class have to raise to completely fence in the playground?
   a. $165.12
   b. $170.59
   c. $183.57
   d. $220.25

39. 160%=
   a. 5/6
   b. 6/5
   c. 8/5
   d. 9/6

40. A solution contains 6% calcium. How many milliliters of solution can be made from 50 ml of calcium?
   a. 833
   b. 952
   c. 1054
   d. 2000

41. 8.7 x 23.3 equals:
   a. 202.71
   b. 2027.1
   c. 212.71
   d. 2127.1

42. 134.5 Divided by 5 equals:
   a. 26.9
   b. 25.9
   c. 23.9
   d. 22.9

43. 5.30×10^{-4} equals:
   a. 000053
   b. 00053
   c. 53,000
   d. 5,300,000

44. 23/3 =
   a. 6 2/3
   b. 7 1/3
   c. 7 2/3
   d. 8 1/3

45. 33/100 =
   a. 0.0033
   b. 0.033
   c. 0.33
   d. 3.3

46. $45^x/5^x$ =
   a. 9^x
   b. 9
   c. 11^x
   d. 11

47. 24x/3 =
   a. 8x
   b. 8
   c. 7x
   d. 7

48. 52x(4y) =
   a. 13xy
   b. 13xy
   c. $208x^{-y}$
   d. 208xy

49. 4500 + 3422 + 3909 =
   a. 12,831
   b. 12,731
   c. 11,831
   d. 11,731

Answer Key for Mathematics Practice 2

1. B: $(500 \times .75) = 375$

2. C: $(600 \times .45) = 270$

3. A: $(35 + 16 = 51)$

4. D: $(4 \times 4 = 16)$

5. D: (31 is a prime number; it is only divisible by itself and one)

6. D: (A factor is a number that divides evenly into another number.)

7. C: $(75 \times 34 = 2550)$

8. B: $(853 - 372 = 481)$

9. A

10. A: $(60 \times 15 = 900)$

11. C: $(15/2)(10/2) = 150/4 = 37.5$

12. C: $(144) + (-6) = 138$

13. B: $(85/100)$ reduces to $17/20$

14. B: Divide all fractions into decimals and compare

15. B: $(72 \times .21 = 15.12)$ $15.12 + 72 = 87.12 \approx 87$ pints

16. B: $(2 \times 2 \times 2 \times 2)(5) = 16 \times 5 = 80$

17. B: (360 degrees ÷ 3 = 120 degrees)

18. C: $(\$25 + \$52 + \$52 + \$34 = \$163)$ $\$163 \div 4 = \$40.75$

19. A: $(437.65 - 325.752 = 111.898)$

20. A: $(43.3 \times 23.03 = 997.199)$

21. C: $(2 \times 2 = 4)$, $(8 \times 24 = 192)$ $192 \text{ in}^2 \div 4 \text{ in}^2 = 48$

22. D: $(157 \text{ lbs} \times .06 = 9.42 \text{ lbs})$ $157 \text{lbs} - 9.42 \text{ lbs} = 147.58 \text{lbs}$

23. B: (650 students x .65 = 422.5) 422.5 – 340 = 82.5 ≈ 83 more students

24. C: (15/100 = 12.75/x) 15x= (100) (12.75) x= 1275/15 = $85

25. B: (Divide out all fractions and compare decimal equivalents)

26. C: (the hundredths place is two right of the decimal point)

27. A: (to get one multiple any fraction by its reciprocal)

28. A: (4 + 6 – (4 + 4) = 2 (work inside of the parentheses first

29. C: (300mg + 120 mg + 900mg + 900mg + 1500mg = 4840mg, 4840mg ÷ 5 = 968 mg

30. C: (6.982 rounds to 7.0) look at the 8 it rounds the 9 to a 10 which adds a one to the ones place, the 0 holds the tenths place

31. B: (.042 x 328 = 13.8)

32. C: (change into fraction form 625/1000 then reduce)

33. C: (multiply everything within the parentheses only)

34. A: Break 80 down into (16) (5), 16 has a square root of 4 leaving 5

35. C: (50 x 60 = 3000)

36. D: (15 + 12 + 17= 44)

37. D: (50 x .1 = 5), 50+5=55, (60 x .1 = 6), 60 + 6 = 66, 66 x 55 = 3630 square yards

38. B: (60 + 60 + 50 + 50 = 220), (220 yards x $15/ yard = $3,300) (3,300 – 400= 2,900), (2,900 ÷17 = $170.59)

39. C: (8/5 = 1.6) 1.6 x 100 = 160%

40. A: (set up a ratio of 6/100 = 50/x) then solve by cross multiplying

41. A: Straight multiplication

42. A: Straight division

43. B: $^{-4}$ Value moves decimal to the left four places.

44. C: 7 2/3

45. C: 33 Divided by 100 = 0.33

46. A: 5^x cancels out.

47. A: Exponents do not cancel out.

48. D: Straight multiplication of numbers and exponents

49. C: Straight addition

Verbal Practice 2

Pick the word that is most appropriate.

1. Susan's _____ of darkness prevents her from leaving her house at night. means
   a. Abhorance
   b. Abhorence
   c. Abhorrence
   d. Abhorrance

2. The girl displayed _____ behavior when she found out her puppy was injured.
   a. Destraught
   b. Distaught
   c. Distraught
   d. Distrauht

3. The French exchange student spoke English as if it were her first language. She was
   a. Dandy
   b. Fluent
   c. Caustic
   d. Talented

4. The prescription plan did not cover name brand drugs if there was a _____ substitute available.
   a. Generic
   b. Reasonable
   c. Compatible
   d. Complete

5. The _____ crowd mourned the loss of their leader.
   a. Sember
   b. Somber
   c. Sombar
   d. Sombor

6. The southern _____ girl was known for her behavior.
   a. Gentell
   b. Ganteel
   c. Genteal
   d. Genteel

7. The mother attempted to _____ her son with toys.
   a. Molifey
   b. Mollify
   c. Molify
   d. Mollifey

8. The car accident caused a sliver of glass to cut the passenger's optic nerve. The passenger lost his
   a. Arm
   b. Movement
   c. Smell
   d. Vision

9. Some people accused John of thinking too much. He would sometimes ___ on a subject for months at a time.
   a. Pondar
   b. Pondder
   c. Ponnder
   d. Ponder

10. The young artist had an _____ passion for watercolors.
    a. Unbradled
    b. Unbriddled
    c. Unbridled
    d. Unbridlled

11. The _____ kept the students cool while they sat outside studying.
    a. Zephyir
    b. Zepheyer
    c. Zepyr
    d. Zephyr

12. The pianist played his rendition of a _____.
    a. Sonata
    b. Sonatina
    c. Sonate
    d. Sonete

13. The entertainer had no _____ about performing in front of two thousand screaming fans.
    a. Qulams
    b. Quelms
    c. Qualms
    d. Qualmes

14. The _____ still enjoyed being around its mother but was acting more independent each day.
    a. Yearling
    b. Yeerling
    c. Yearlling
    d. Yearlinng

- 75 -

15. The financial planner had reached the top of his career; he felt he was at his
    a. Performance
    b. Stress level
    c. Limit
    d. Zenith

16. The siblings found _____ in each other as they ___ the good times with their father.
    a. Happiness, Prepared
    b. Sorrow, Committed
    c. Solace, Remembered
    d. Sorrow, Limited

17. The young boy sat _____ as the principal yelled at him.
    a. Passivly
    b. Pasively
    c. Passivelly
    d. Passively

18. The teenage was accused of killing his father and mother. He was accused of
    a. Sobriety
    b. Misguidance
    c. Misgamy
    d. Parricide

19. Brian's secret to studying success relied on a system designed to assist with the recollection of terms. His secret was the use of
    a. Syllables
    b. Memorabilia
    c. Mnemonics
    d. Puzzles

Identify the appropriate error in the following sentences.

20. The bachalor never married. Most people thought it was because of misogyny.
    a. Capitalization
    b. Punctuation
    c. Spelling
    d. Grammar

21. The intricacy of the mathematical equation, drove the student crazy trying to solve it.
    a. Capitalization
    b. Punctuation
    c. Spelling
    d. Grammar

22. The hybrid tomatoes is immune to most common diseases.
    a. Capitalization
    b. Punctuation
    c. Spelling
    d. Grammar

23. The professor was humiliated when his students reported him to the Dean for verbal abuse.
    a. Capitalization
    b. Punctuation
    c. Spelling
    d. Grammar

24. The con artist hoodwinked the old lady when he sold her fradulent insurance.
    a. Capitalization
    b. Punctuation
    c. Spelling
    d. Grammar

25. The movie star was accused of a misdemeanor, when she stole 15 dollars worth of merchandise from the store.
    a. Capitalization
    b. Punctuation
    c. Spelling
    d. Grammar

26. The congregation sang a comtemporary hymn.
    a. Capitalization
    b. Punctuation
    c. Spelling
    d. Grammar

Answer Key for Verbal Practice 2

1. C
2. C
3. B
4. A
5. B
6. D
7. B
8. D
9. D
10. C
11. D
12. A
13. C
14. A
15. D
16. C
17. D
18. D
19. C
20. C
21. B
22. D
23. A
24. C
25. B
26. C

Secret Key #1 – Time is Your Greatest Enemy

To succeed on the Wonderlic exam, you must use your time wisely. Most test takers do not finish the entire test. To succeed, you must ration your time properly. The reason that time is so critical is that every question counts the same toward your final score. There are 30 questions on the exam and you only have 8 minutes. 16 seconds per question.

Success Strategy #1

Pace Yourself

Wear a watch to the Wonderlic exam. At the beginning of the test, check the time (or start a chronometer on your watch to count the minutes), and check the time after every few questions to make sure you are "on schedule."

If you find that you are falling behind time during the test, you must speed up. Even though a rushed answer is more likely to be incorrect, it is better to miss a couple of questions by being rushed, than to completely miss later questions by not having enough time. It is better to end with more time than you need than to run out of time.

If you are forced to speed up, do it efficiently. Usually one or more answer choices can be eliminated without too much difficulty. Above all, don't panic. Don't speed up and just begin guessing at random choices. By pacing yourself, and continually monitoring your progress against your watch, you will always know exactly how far ahead or behind you are with your available time. If you find that you are a few minutes behind on a section, don't skip questions without spending any time on it, just to catch back up. Begin spending a little less time per question and after a few questions, you will have caught back up more gradually. Once you catch back up, you can continue working each problem at your normal pace. If you have time at the end, go back then and finish the questions that you left behind.

Furthermore, don't dwell on the problems that you were rushed on. If a problem was taking up too much time and you made a hurried guess, it must have been difficult. The difficult questions are the ones you are most likely to miss anyway, so it isn't a big loss. If you have time left over, as you review the skipped questions, start at the earliest skipped question, spend at most another minute, and then move on to the next skipped question.

Lastly, sometimes it is beneficial to slow down if you are constantly getting ahead of time. You are always more likely to catch a careless mistake by working more slowly than quickly, and among very high-scoring test takers (those who are likely to have lots of time left over), careless errors affect the score more than mastery of material.

Secret Key #2 – Guessing is not Guesswork

Most test takers do not understand the impact that proper guessing can have on their score. Unless you score extremely high, guessing will contribute a significant amount of points to your score.

Success Strategy #2

Let me introduce one of the most valuable ideas of this course- the $5 challenge:

You only mark your "best guess" if you are willing to bet $5 on it.
You only eliminate choices from guessing if you are willing to bet $5 on it.

Why $5? Five dollars is an amount of money that is small yet not insignificant, and can really add up fast (20 questions could cost you $100). Likewise, each answer choice on one question of the Wonderlic exam will have a small impact on your overall score, but it can really add up to a lot of points in the end.

The process of elimination IS valuable. The following shows your chance of guessing it right:

If you eliminate this many choices:	0	1	2	3
Chance of getting it correct	25%	33%	50%	100%

However, if you accidentally eliminate the right answer or go on a hunch for an incorrect answer, your chances drop dramatically: to 0%. By guessing among all the answer choices, you are GUARANTEED to have a shot at the right answer.

That's why the $5 test is so valuable- if you give up the advantage and safety of a pure guess, it had better be worth the risk.

What we still haven't covered is how to be sure that whatever guess you make is truly random. Here's the easiest way:

Always pick the first answer choice among those remaining.

Such a technique means that you have decided, **before you see a single test question**, exactly how you are going to guess- and since the order of choices tells you nothing about which one is correct, this guessing technique is perfectly random.

This section is not meant to scare you away from making educated guesses or eliminating choices- you just need to define when a choice is worth eliminating. The $5 test, along with a pre-defined random guessing strategy, is the best way to make sure you reap all of the benefits of guessing.

Specific Guessing Techniques

Similar Answer Choices

When you have two answer choices that are direct opposites, one of them is usually the correct answer.
Example:
A. forward
B. backward

These two answer choices are very similar and fall into the same family of
answer choices. A family of answer choices is when two or three answer choices are very similar. Often two will be opposites and one may show an equality.
Example:
A. excited
B. overjoyed
C. thrilled
D. upset

Note how the first three choices are all related. They all ask describe a state of happiness. However, choice D is not in the same family of questions. Being upset is the direct opposite of happiness.

Summary of Guessing Techniques

1. Eliminate as many choices as you can by using the $5 test. Use the common guessing strategies to help in the elimination process, but only eliminate choices that pass the $5 test.
2. Among the remaining choices, only pick your "best guess" if it passes the $5 test.
3. Otherwise, guess randomly by picking the first remaining choice that was not eliminated.

Secret Key #3 – Practice Smarter, Not Harder

Many test takers delay the test preparation process because they dread the awful amounts of practice time they think necessary to succeed on the test. We have refined an effective method that will take you only a fraction of the time.

There are a number of "obstacles" in your way on the Wonderlic exam. Among these are answering questions, finishing in time, and mastering test-taking strategies. All must be executed on the day of the test at peak performance, or your score will suffer. The Wonderlic exam is a quick mental marathon that has a large impact on your future.

Just like a marathon runner, it is important to work your way up to the full challenge. So first you just worry about questions, and then time, and finally strategy:

Success Strategy #3

1. Find a good source for math and verbal practice tests.
2. If you are willing to make a larger time investment (or if you want to really "learn" the material, a time consuming but ultimately valuable endeavor), consider buying one of the better study guides on the market
3. Take a practice test with no time constraints, with all study helps "open book." Take your time with questions and focus on applying the strategies.
4. Take another test, this time with time constraints, with all study helps "open book."
5. Take a final practice test with no open material and time limits.

If you have time to take more practice tests, just repeat step 5. By gradually exposing yourself to the full rigors of the test environment, you will condition your mind to the stress of test day and maximize your success.

Secret Key #4 — Prepare, Don't Procrastinate

Let me state an obvious fact: if you take the Wonderlic exam three times, you will get three different scores. This is due to the way you feel on test day, the level of preparedness you have, and, despite Wonderlic exam's claims to the contrary, some tests WILL be easier for you than others.

Since your acceptance will largely depend on your score, you should maximize your chances of success. In order to maximize the likelihood of success, you've got to prepare in advance. This means taking practice tests and spending time learning the information and test taking strategies you will need to succeed.

Since you have to pay a registration fee each time you take the Wonderlic exam, don't take it as a "practice" test. Feel free to take sample tests on your own, but when you go to take the Wonderlic exam, be prepared, be focused, and do your best the first time!

Secret Key #5 – Test Yourself

Everyone knows that time is money. Many test takers take too little time preparing for the Wonderlic exam. You should spend as much of your precious time preparing that is necessary for you to ace it.

Success Strategy #5

Once you have taken a practice test under real conditions of time constraints, then you will know if you are ready for the test or not.

If you have scored extremely high the first time that you take the practice test, then there is not much point in spending countless hours studying. You are already there.

Benchmark your abilities by retaking practice tests and seeing how much you have improved. Once you score high enough to get accepted into the school of your choice, then you are ready.

If you have scored well below where you need, then knuckle down and begin studying in earnest. Check your improvement regularly through the use of practice tests under real conditions. Above all, don't worry, panic, or give up. The key is perseverance!

Then, when you go to take the Wonderlic exam, remain confident and remember how well you did on the practice tests. If you can score high enough on a practice test, then you can do the same on the real thing.

General Strategies

The most important thing you can do is to ignore your fears and jump into the test immediately- do not be overwhelmed by any strange-sounding terms. You have to jump into the test like jumping into a pool- all at once is the easiest way.

Make Predictions

As you read and understand the question, try to guess what the answer will be. Remember that several of the answer choices are wrong, and once you begin reading them, your mind will immediately become cluttered with answer choices designed to throw you off. Your mind is typically the most focused immediately after you have read the question and digested its contents. If you can, try to predict what the correct answer will be. You may be surprised at what you can predict.

Quickly scan the choices and see if your prediction is in the listed answer choices. If it is, then you can be quite confident that you have the right answer. It still won't hurt to check the other answer choices, but most of the time, you've got it!

Answer the Question

It may seem obvious to only pick answer choices that answer the question, but the test writers can create some excellent answer choices that are wrong. Don't pick an answer just because it sounds right, or you believe it to be true. It MUST answer the question. Once you've made your selection, always go back and check it against the question and make sure that you didn't misread the question, and the answer choice does answer the question posed.

Benchmark

After you read the first answer choice, decide if you think it sounds correct or not. If it doesn't, move on to the next answer choice. If it does, mentally mark that answer choice. This doesn't mean that you've definitely selected it as your answer choice, it just means that it's the best you've seen thus far. Go ahead and read the next choice. If the next choice is worse than the one you've already selected, keep going to the next answer choice. If the next choice is better than the choice you've already selected, mentally mark the new answer choice as your best guess.

The first answer choice that you select becomes your standard. Every other answer choice must be benchmarked against that standard. That choice is correct until proven otherwise by another answer choice beating it out. Once you've decided that no other answer choice seems as good, do one final check to ensure that your answer choice answers the question posed.

Valid Information

Don't discount any of the information provided in the question. Every piece of information may be necessary to determine the correct answer. None of the information in the question is there to throw you off (while the answer choices will certainly have information to throw you off). If two seemingly unrelated topics are discussed, don't ignore either. You can be confident there is a relationship, or it wouldn't be included in the question, and you are probably going to have to determine what that relationship is to find the answer.

Avoid "Fact Traps"

Don't get distracted by a choice that is factually true. Your search is for the answer that answers the question. Stay focused and don't fall for an answer that is true but incorrect. Always go back to the question and make sure you're choosing an answer that actually answers the question and is not just a true statement. An answer can be factually correct, but it MUST answer the question asked. Additionally, two answers can both be seemingly correct, so be sure to read all of the answer choices, and make sure that you get the one that BEST answers the question.

Milk the Question

Some of the questions may throw you completely off. They might deal with a subject you have not been exposed to, or one that you haven't reviewed in years. While your lack of knowledge about the subject will be a hindrance, the question itself can give you many clues that will help you find the correct answer. Read the question carefully and look for clues. Watch particularly for adjectives and nouns describing difficult terms or words that you don't recognize. Regardless of if you completely understand a word or not, replacing it with a synonym either provided or one you more familiar with may help you to understand what the questions are asking. Rather than wracking your mind about specific detailed information concerning a difficult term or word, try to use mental substitutes that are easier to understand.

The Trap of Familiarity

Don't just choose a word because you recognize it. On difficult questions, you may not recognize a number of words in the answer choices. The test writers don't put "make-believe" words on the test; so don't think that just because you only recognize all the words in one answer choice means that answer choice must be correct. If you only recognize words in one answer choice, then focus on that one. Is it correct? Try your best to determine if it is correct. If it is that is great; but, if it doesn't, eliminate it. Each word and answer choice you eliminate increases your chances of getting the question correct, even if you then have to guess among the unfamiliar choices.

Eliminate Answers

Eliminate choices as soon as you realize they are wrong. But be careful! Make sure you consider all of the possible answer choices. Just because one appears right, doesn't mean that the next one won't be even better! The test writers will usually put more than one good answer choice for every question, so read all of them. Don't worry if you are stuck between two that seem right. By getting down to just two remaining possible choices, your odds are now 50/50.

Rather than wasting too much time, play the odds. You are guessing, but guessing wisely, because you've been able to knock out some of the answer choices that you know are wrong. If you are eliminating choices and realize that the last answer choice you are left with is also obviously wrong, don't panic. Start over and consider each choice again. There may easily be something that you missed the first time and will realize on the second pass.

Tough Questions

If you are stumped on a problem or it appears too hard or too difficult, don't waste time. Move on! Remember though, if you can quickly check for obviously incorrect answer choices, your chances of guessing correctly are greatly improved. Before you completely give up, at least try to knock out a couple of possible answers. Eliminate what you can and then guess at the remaining answer choices before moving on.

Brainstorm

If you get stuck on a difficult question, spend a few seconds quickly brainstorming. Run through the complete list of possible answer choices. Look at each choice and ask yourself, "Could this answer the question satisfactorily?" Go through each answer choice and consider it independently of the other. By systematically going through all possibilities, you may find something that you would otherwise overlook. Remember that when you get stuck, it's important to try to keep moving.

Read Carefully

Understand the problem. Read the question and answer choices carefully. Don't miss the question because you misread the terms. You have plenty of time to read each question thoroughly and make sure you understand what is being asked. Yet a happy medium must be attained, so don't waste too much time. You must read carefully, but efficiently.

Face Value

When in doubt, use common sense. Always accept the situation in the problem at face value. Don't read too much into it. These problems will not require you to make huge leaps of logic. The test writers aren't trying to throw you off with a cheap trick. If you have to go beyond creativity and make a leap of logic in order to have an answer choice answer the question, then you should look at the other answer choices. Don't overcomplicate the problem by creating theoretical relationships or explanations that will warp time or space. These are normal problems rooted in reality. It's just that the applicable relationship or explanation may not be readily apparent and you have to figure things out. Use your common sense to interpret anything that isn't clear.

Prefixes

If you're having trouble with a word in the question or answer choices, try dissecting it. Take advantage of every clue that the word might include. Prefixes and suffixes can be a huge help. Usually they allow you to determine a basic meaning. Pre- means before, post-means after, pro - is positive, de- is negative. From these prefixes and suffixes, you can get an idea of the general meaning of the word and try to put it into context. Beware though of any traps. Just because con is the opposite of pro, doesn't necessarily mean congress is the opposite of progress!

Hedge Phrases

Watch out for critical "hedge" phrases, such as likely, may, can, will often, sometimes, often, almost, mostly, usually, generally, rarely, sometimes. Question writers insert these hedge phrases to cover every possibility. Often an answer choice will be wrong simply because it leaves no room for exception. Avoid answer choices that have definitive words like "exactly," and "always".

Switchback Words

Stay alert for "switchbacks". These are the words and phrases frequently used to alert you to shifts in thought. The most common switchback word is "but". Others include although, however, nevertheless, on the other hand, even though, while, in spite of, despite, regardless of.

New Information

Correct answer choices will rarely have completely new information included. Answer choices typically are straightforward reflections of the material asked about and will directly relate to the question. If a new piece of information is included in an answer choice that doesn't even seem to relate to the topic being asked about, then that answer choice is likely incorrect. All of the information needed to answer the question is usually provided for you, and so you should not have to make guesses that are unsupported or choose answer choices that require unknown information that cannot be reasoned on its own.

Time Management

On technical questions, don't get lost on the technical terms. Don't spend too much time on any one question. If you don't know what a term means, then since you don't have a dictionary, odds are you aren't going to get much further. You should immediately recognize terms as whether or not you know them. If you don't, work with the other clues that you have, the other answer choices and terms provided, but don't waste too much time trying to figure out a difficult term.

Contextual Clues

Look for contextual clues. An answer can be right but not correct. The contextual clues will help you find the answer that is most right and is correct. Understand the context in which a phrase or statement is made. This will help you make important distinctions.

Don't Panic

Panicking will not answer any questions for you. Therefore, it isn't helpful. When you first see the question, if your mind goes blank, take a deep breath. Force yourself to mechanically go through the steps of solving the problem and using the strategies you've learned.

Pace Yourself

Don't get clock fever. It's easy to be overwhelmed when you're looking at a page full of questions, your mind is full of random thoughts and feeling confused, and the clock is ticking down faster than you would like. Calm down and maintain the pace that you have set for yourself. As long as you are on track by monitoring your pace, you are guaranteed to have enough time for yourself. When you get to the last few minutes of the test, it may seem like you won't have enough time left, but if you only have as many questions as you should have left at that point, then you're right on track!

Answer Selection

The best way to pick an answer choice is to eliminate all of those that are wrong, until only one is left and confirm that is the correct answer. Sometimes though, an answer choice may immediately look right. Be careful! Take a second to make sure that the other choices are not equally obvious. Don't make a hasty mistake. There are only two times that you should stop before checking other answers. First is when you are positive that the answer choice you have selected is correct. Second is when time is almost out and you have to make a quick guess!

Check Your Work

Since you will probably not know every term listed and the answer to every question, it is important that you get credit for the ones that you do know. Don't miss any questions through careless mistakes. If at all possible, try to take a second to look back over your answer selection and make sure you've selected the correct answer choice and haven't made a costly careless mistake (such as marking an answer choice that you didn't mean to mark). This quick double check should more than pay for itself in caught mistakes for the time it costs.

Beware of Directly Quoted Answers

Sometimes an answer choice will repeat word for word a portion of the question or reference section. However, beware of such exact duplication – it may be a trap! More than likely, the correct choice will paraphrase or summarize a point, rather than being exactly the same wording.

Slang

Scientific sounding answers are better than slang ones. An answer choice that begins "To compare the outcomes..." is much more likely to be correct than one that begins "Because some people insisted..."

Extreme Statements

Avoid wild answers that throw out highly controversial ideas that are proclaimed as established fact. An answer choice that states the "process should be used in certain situations, if..." is much more likely to be correct than one that states the "process should be discontinued completely." The first is a calm rational statement and doesn't even make a definitive, uncompromising stance, using a hedge word "if" to provide wiggle room, whereas the second choice is a radical idea and far more extreme.

Answer Choice Families

When you have two or more answer choices that are direct opposites or parallels, one of them is usually the correct answer. For instance, if one answer choice states "x increases" and another answer choice states "x decreases" or "y increases," then those two or three answer choices are very similar in construction and fall into the same family of answer choices. A family of answer choices is when two or three answer choices are very similar in construction, and yet often have a directly opposite meaning. Usually the correct answer choice will be in that family of answer choices. The "odd man out" or answer choice that doesn't seem to fit the parallel construction of the other answer choices is more likely to be incorrect.

Special Report: How to Overcome Test Anxiety

The very nature of tests caters to some level of anxiety, nervousness or tension, just as we feel for any important event that occurs in our lives. A little bit of anxiety or nervousness can be a good thing. It helps us with motivation, and makes achievement just that much sweeter. However, too much anxiety can be a problem; especially if it hinders our ability to function and perform.

"Test anxiety," is the term that refers to the emotional reactions that some test-takers experience when faced with a test or exam. Having a fear of testing and exams is based upon a rational fear, since the test-taker's performance can shape the course of an academic career. Nevertheless, experiencing excessive fear of examinations will only interfere with the test-takers ability to perform, and his/her chances to be successful.

There are a large variety of causes that can contribute to the development and sensation of test anxiety. These include, but are not limited to lack of performance and worrying about issues surrounding the test.

Lack of Preparation

Lack of preparation can be identified by the following behaviors or situations:

Not scheduling enough time to study, and therefore cramming the night before the test or exam
Managing time poorly, to create the sensation that there is not enough time to do everything
Failing to organize the text information in advance, so that the study material consists of the entire text and not simply the pertinent information
Poor overall studying habits

Worrying, on the other hand, can be related to either the test taker, or many other factors around him/her that will be affected by the results of the test. These include worrying about:

Previous performances on similar exams, or exams in general
How friends and other test takers are achieving
The negative consequences that will result from a poor grade or failure

There are three primary elements to test anxiety: 1) Physical components, which involve the same typical bodily reactions as those to acute anxiety (to be discussed below). 2) Emotional factors have to do with fear or panic, and 3) Mental or cognitive issues concerning attention spans and memory abilities.

Physical Signals

There are many different symptoms of test anxiety, and these are not limited to mental and emotional strain. Frequently there are a range of physical signals that will let a test taker know that he/she is suffering from test anxiety. These bodily changes can include the following:

Perspiring
Sweaty palms
Wet, trembling hands
Nausea
Dry mouth
A knot in the stomach
Headache
Faintness
Muscle tension
Aching shoulders, back and neck
Rapid heart beat
Feeling too hot/cold
To recognize the sensation of test anxiety, a test-taker should monitor him/herself for the following sensations:
- The physical distress symptoms as listed above
- Emotional sensitivity, expressing emotional feelings such as the need to cry or laugh too much, or a sensation of anger or helplessness
- A decreased ability to think, causing the test-taker to blank out or have racing thoughts that are hard to organize or control.

Though most test takers will feel some level of anxiety when faced with a test or exam, the majority can cope with that anxiety and maintain it at a manageable level. However, those who cannot are faced with a very real and very serious condition, which can and should be controlled for the immeasurable benefit of this sufferer.

Naturally, these sensations lead to negative results for the testing experience. The most common effects of test anxiety have to do with nervousness and mental blocking.

Nervousness

Nervousness can appear in several different levels:

The test-taker's difficulty, or even inability to read and understand the questions on the test
The difficulty or inability to organize thoughts to a coherent form
The difficulty or inability to recall key words and concepts relating to the testing questions (especially essays)
The receipt of poor grades on a test, though the test material was well known by the test taker

Conversely, a person may also experience mental blocking, which involves:
- Blanking out on test questions
- Only remembering the correct answers to the questions when the test has already finished.

Fortunately for test anxiety sufferers, beating these feelings, to a large degree, has to do with proper preparation. When a test taker has a feeling of preparedness, then anxiety will be dramatically lessened.

The first step to resolving anxiety issues is to distinguish which of the two types of anxiety are being suffered. If the anxiety is a direct result of a lack of preparation, this should be considered a normal reaction, and the anxiety level (as opposed to the test results) shouldn't be anything to worry about. However, if, when adequately prepared, the test-taker still panics, blanks out, or seems to overreact, this is not a fully rational reaction. While this can be considered normal too, there are many ways to combat and overcome these effects.

Remember that anxiety cannot be entirely eliminated; however, there are ways to minimize it, to make the anxiety easier to manage. Preparation is one of the best ways to minimize test anxiety. Therefore the following techniques are wise in order to best fight off any anxiety that may want to build.

To begin with, try to avoid cramming before a test, whenever it is possible. By trying to memorize an entire term's worth of information in one day, you'll be shocking your system, and not giving yourself a very good chance to absorb the information. This is an easy path to anxiety, so for those who suffer from test anxiety, cramming should not even be considered an option.

Instead of cramming, work throughout the semester to combine all of the material which is presented throughout the semester, and work on it gradually as the course goes by, making sure to master the main concepts first, leaving minor details for a week or so before the test.

To study for the upcoming exam, be sure to pose questions that may be on the examination, to gauge the ability to answer them by integrating the ideas from your texts, notes and lectures, as well as any supplementary readings.

If it is truly impossible to cover all of the information that was covered in that particular term, concentrate on the most important portions, that can be covered very well. Learn these concepts as best as possible, so that when the test comes, a goal can be made to use these concepts as presentations of your knowledge.

In addition to study habits, changes in attitude are critical to beating a struggle with test anxiety. In fact, an improvement of the perspective over the entire test-taking experience can actually help a test taker to enjoy studying and therefore improve the overall experience. Be certain not to overemphasize the significance of the grade - know that the result of the test is neither a reflection of self worth, nor is it a measure of intelligence; one grade will not predict a person's future success.

To improve an overall testing outlook, the following steps should be tried:

Keeping in mind that the most reasonable expectation for taking a test is to expect to try to demonstrate as much of what you know as you possibly can.
Reminding ourselves that a test is only one test; this is not the only one, and there will be others.
The thought of thinking of oneself in an irrational, all-or-nothing term should be avoided at all costs.
A reward should be designated for after the test, so there's something to look forward to. Whether it be going to a movie, going out to eat, or simply visiting friends, schedule it in advance, and do it no matter what result is expected on the exam.

Test-takers should also keep in mind that the basics are some of the most important things, even beyond anti-anxiety techniques and studying. Never neglect the basic social, emotional and biological needs, in order to try to absorb information. In order to best achieve, these three factors must be held as just as important as the studying itself.

Study Steps

Remember the following important steps for studying:

- Maintain healthy nutrition and exercise habits. Continue both your recreational activities and social pass times. These both contribute to your physical and emotional well being.
- Be certain to get a good amount of sleep, especially the night before the test, because when you're overtired you are not able to perform to the best of your best ability.
- Keep the studying pace to a moderate level by taking breaks when they are needed, and varying the work whenever possible, to keep the mind fresh instead of getting bored.
- When enough studying has been done that all the material that can be learned has been learned, and the test taker is prepared for the test, stop studying and do something relaxing such as listening to music, watching a movie, or taking a warm bubble bath.

There are also many other techniques to minimize the uneasiness or apprehension that is experienced along with test anxiety before, during, or even after the examination. In fact, there are a great deal of things that can be done to stop anxiety from interfering with lifestyle and performance. Again, remember that anxiety will not be eliminated entirely, and it shouldn't be. Otherwise that "up" feeling for exams would not exist, and most of us depend on that sensation to perform better than usual. However, this anxiety has to be at a level that is manageable.

Of course, as we have just discussed, being prepared for the exam is half the battle right away. Attending all classes, finding out what knowledge will be expected on the exam, and knowing the exam schedules are easy steps to lowering anxiety. Keeping up with work will remove the need to cram, and efficient study habits will eliminate wasted time. Studying should be done in an ideal location for concentration, so that it is simple to become interested in the material and give it complete attention.

A method such as SQ3R (Survey, Question, Read, Recite, Review) is a wonderful key to follow to make sure that the study habits are as effective as possible, especially in the case of learning from a textbook. Flashcards are great techniques for memorization. Learning to take good notes will mean that notes will be full of useful information, so that less sifting will need to be done to seek out what is pertinent for studying. Reviewing notes after class and then again on occasion will keep the information fresh in the mind. From notes that have been taken summary sheets and outlines can be made for simpler reviewing.
A study group can also be a very motivational and helpful place to study, as there will be a sharing of ideas, all of the minds can work together, to make sure that everyone understands, and the studying will be made more interesting because it will be a social occasion.

Basically, though, as long as the test-taker remains organized and self confident, with efficient study habits, less time will need to be spent studying, and higher grades will be achieved.

To become self-confident, there are many useful steps. The first of these is "self talk." It has been shown through extensive research, that self-talk for test takers who suffer from test anxiety, should be well monitored, in order to make sure that it contributes to self confidence as opposed to sinking the student. Frequently the self talk of test-anxious test takers is negative or self-defeating, thinking that everyone else is smarter and faster, that they always mess up, and that if they don't do well, they'll fail the entire course. It is important to decreasing anxiety that awareness is made of self talk. Try writing any negative self thoughts and then disputing them with a positive statement instead. Begin self-encouragement as though it was a friend speaking. Repeat positive statements to help reprogram the mind to believing in successes instead of failures.

Helpful Techniques

Other extremely helpful techniques include:

- Self-visualization of doing well and reaching goals
- While aiming for an "A" level of understanding, don't try to "overprotect" by setting your expectations lower. This will only convince the mind to stop studying in order to meet the lower expectations.
- Don't make comparisons with the results or habits of other test takers. These are individual factors, and different things work for different people, causing different results.
- Strive to become an expert in learning what works well, and what can be done in order to improve. Consider collecting this data in a journal.
- Create rewards for after studying instead of doing things before studying that will only turn into avoidance behaviors.
- Make a practice of relaxing - by using methods such as progressive relaxation, self-hypnosis, guided imagery, etc - in order to make relaxation an automatic sensation.

- Work on creating a state of relaxed concentration so that concentrating will take on the focus of the mind, so that none will be wasted on worrying.
- Take good care of the physical self by eating well and getting enough sleep.
- Plan in time for exercise and stick to this plan.

Beyond these techniques, there are other methods to be used before, during and after the test that will help the test-taker perform well in addition to overcoming anxiety.

Before the exam comes the academic preparation. This involves establishing a study schedule and beginning at least one week before the actual date of the test. By doing this, the anxiety of not having enough time to study for the test will be automatically eliminated. Moreover, this will make the studying a much more effective experience, ensuring that the learning will be an easier process. This relieves much undue pressure on the test-taker.

Summary sheets, note cards, and flash cards with the main concepts and examples of these main concepts should be prepared in advance of the actual studying time. A topic should never be eliminated from this process. By omitting a topic because it isn't expected to be on the test is only setting up the test-taker for anxiety should it actually appear on the exam. Utilize the course syllabus for laying out the topics that should be studied. Carefully go over the notes that were made in class, paying special attention to any of the issues that the professor took special care to emphasize while lecturing in class. In the textbooks, use the chapter review, or if possible, the chapter tests, to begin your review.

It may even be possible to ask the instructor what information will be covered on the exam, or what the format of the exam will be (for example, multiple choice, essay, free form, true-false). Additionally, see if it is possible to find out how many questions will be on the test. If a review sheet or sample test has been offered by the professor, make good use of it, above anything else, for the preparation for the test. Another great resource for getting to know the examination is reviewing tests from previous semesters. Use these tests to review, and aim to achieve a 100% score on each of the possible topics. With a few exceptions, the goal that you set for yourself is the highest one that you will reach.

Take all of the questions that were assigned as homework, and rework them to any other possible course material. The more problems reworked, the more skill and confidence will form as a result. When forming the solution to a problem, write out each of the steps. Don't simply do head work. By doing as many steps on paper as possible, much clarification and therefore confidence will be formed. Do this with as many homework problems as possible, before checking the answers. By checking the answer after each problem, a reinforcement will exist, that will not be on the exam. Study situations should be as exam-like as possible, to prime the test-taker's system for the experience. By waiting to check the answers at the end, a psychological advantage will be formed, to decrease the stress factor.

Another fantastic reason for not cramming is the avoidance of confusion in concepts, especially when it comes to mathematics. 8-10 hours of study will become one hundred percent more effective if it is spread out over a week or at least several days, instead of doing it all in one sitting. Recognize that the human brain requires time in order to assimilate new material, so frequent breaks and a span of study time over several days will be much more beneficial.

Additionally, don't study right up until the point of the exam. Studying should stop a minimum of one hour before the exam begins. This allows the brain to rest and put things in their proper order. This will also provide the time to become as relaxed as possible when going into the examination room. The test-taker will also have time to eat well and eat sensibly. Know that the brain needs food as much as the rest of the body. With enough food and enough sleep, as well as a relaxed attitude, the body and the mind are primed for success. Avoid any anxious classmates who are talking about the exam. These test takers only spread anxiety, and are not worth sharing the anxious sentimentalities.

Before the test also involves creating a positive attitude, so mental preparation should also be a point of concentration. There are many keys to creating a positive attitude. Should fears become rushing in, make a visualization of taking the exam, doing well, and seeing an A written on the paper. Write out a list of affirmations that will bring a feeling of confidence, such as "I am doing well in my English class," "I studied well and know my material," "I enjoy this class." Even if the affirmations aren't believed at first, it sends a positive message to the subconscious which will result in an alteration of the overall belief system, which is the system that creates reality.

If a sensation of panic begins, work with the fear and imagine the very worst! Work through the entire scenario of not passing the test, failing the entire course, and dropping out of school, followed by not getting a job, and pushing a shopping cart through the dark alley where you'll live. This will place things into perspective! Then, practice deep breathing and create a visualization of the opposite situation - achieving an "A" on the exam, passing the entire course, receiving the degree at a graduation ceremony.

On the day of the test, there are many things to be done to ensure the best results, as well as the calmest outlook. The following stages are suggested in order to maximize test-taking potential:

- Begin the examination day with a moderate breakfast, and avoid any coffee or beverages with caffeine if the test taker is prone to jitters. Even people who are used to managing caffeine can feel jittery or light-headed when it is taken on a test day.
- Attempt to do something that is relaxing before the examination begins. As last minute cramming clouds the mastering of overall concepts, it is better to use this time to create a calming outlook.
- Be certain to arrive at the test location well in advance, in order to provide time to select a location that is away from doors, windows and other distractions, as well as giving enough time to relax before the test begins.
- Keep away from anxiety generating classmates who will upset the sensation of stability and relaxation that is being attempted before the exam.
- Should the waiting period before the exam begins cause anxiety, create a self-distraction by reading a light magazine or something else that is relaxing and simple.

During the exam itself, read the entire exam from beginning to end, and find out how much time should be allotted to each individual problem. Once writing the exam, should more time be taken for a problem, it should be abandoned, in order to begin another problem. If there is time at the end, the unfinished problem can always be returned to and completed.

Read the instructions very carefully - twice - so that unpleasant surprises won't follow during or after the exam has ended.

When writing the exam, pretend that the situation is actually simply the completion of homework within a library, or at home. This will assist in forming a relaxed atmosphere, and will allow the brain extra focus for the complex thinking function. Begin the exam with all of the questions with which the most confidence is felt. This will build the confidence level regarding the entire exam and will begin a quality momentum. This will also create encouragement for trying the problems where uncertainty resides. Going with the "gut instinct" is always the way to go when solving a problem. Second guessing should be avoided at all costs. Have confidence in the ability to do well.

For essay questions, create an outline in advance that will keep the mind organized and make certain that all of the points are remembered. For multiple choice, read every answer, even if the correct one has been spotted - a better one may exist. Continue at a pace that is reasonable and not rushed, in order to be able to work carefully. Provide enough time to go over the answers at the end, to check for small errors that can be corrected. Should a feeling of panic begin, breathe deeply, and think of the feeling of the body releasing sand through its pores. Visualize a calm, peaceful place, and include all of the sights, sounds and sensations of this image. Continue the deep breathing, and take a few minutes to continue this with closed eyes. When all is well again, return to the test.

If a "blanking" occurs for a certain question, skip it and move on to the next question. There will be time to return to the other question later. Get everything done that can be done, first, to guarantee all the grades that can be compiled, and to build all of the confidence possible. Then return to the weaker questions to build the marks from there. Remember, one's own reality can be created, so as long as the belief is there, success will follow. And remember: anxiety can happen later, right now, there's an exam to be written! After the examination is complete, whether there is a feeling for a good grade or a bad grade, don't dwell on the exam, and be certain to follow through on the reward that was promised...and enjoy it! Don't dwell on any mistakes that have been made, as there is nothing that can be done at this point anyway. Additionally, don't begin to study for the next test right away. Do something relaxing for a while, and let the mind relax and prepare itself to begin absorbing information again.

From the results of the exam - both the grade and the entire experience, be certain to learn from what has gone on. Perfect studying habits and work some more on confidence in order to make the next examination experience even better than the last one. Learn to avoid places where openings occurred for laziness, procrastination and day dreaming.

Use the time between this exam and the next one to learn to relax better (even learning to relax on cue) so that any anxiety can be controlled during the next exam. Learn how to relax the body. Slouch in your chair if that helps. Tighten and then relax all of the different muscle groups, one group at a time, beginning with the feet and then working all the way up to the neck and face. This will ultimately relax the muscles more than they were to begin with. Learn how to breathe deeply and comfortably, and focus on this breathing going in and out as a relaxing thought. With every exhale, repeat the word "relax." As common as test anxiety is, it is very possible to overcome it. Make yourself one of the test-takers who overcome this frustrating hindrance.

Special Report: How to Overcome Your Fear of Math

If this article started by saying "Math," many of us would feel a shiver crawl up our spines, just by reading that simple word. Images of torturous years in those crippling desks of the math classes can become so vivid to our consciousness that we can almost smell those musty textbooks, and see the smudges of the #2 pencils on our fingers.

If you are still a student, feeling the impact of these sometimes overwhelming classroom sensations, you are not alone if you get anxious at just the thought of taking that compulsory math course. Does your heart beat just that much faster when you have to split the bill for lunch among your friends with a group of your friends? Do you truly believe that you simply don't have the brain for math? Certainly you're good at other things, but math just simply isn't one of them? Have you ever avoided activities, or other school courses because they appear to involve mathematics, with which you're simply not comfortable?

If any one or more of these "symptoms" can be applied to you, you could very well be suffering from a very real condition called "Math Anxiety."

It's not at all uncommon for people to think that they have some sort of math disability or allergy, when in actuality, their block is a direct result of the way in which they were taught math!

In the late 1950's with the dawning of the space age, New Math - a new "fuzzy math" reform that focuses on higher-order thinking, conceptual understanding and solving problems - took the country by storm. It's now becoming ever more clear that teachers were not supplied with the correct, practical and effective way in which they should be teaching new math so that test takers will understand the methods comfortably. So is it any wonder that so many test takers struggled so deeply, when their teachers were required to change their entire math systems without the foundation of proper training? Even if you have not been personally, directly affected by that precise event, its impact is still as rampant as ever.

Basically, the math teachers of today are either the teachers who began teaching the new math in the first place (without proper training) or they are the test takers of the math teachers who taught new math without proper training. Therefore, unless they had a unique, exceptional teacher, their primary, consistent examples of teaching math have been teachers using methods that are not conducive to the general understanding of the entire class. This explains why your discomfort (or fear) of math is not at all rare.

It is very clear why being called up to the chalk board to solve a math problem is such a common example of a terrifying situation for test takers - and it has very little to do with a fear of being in front of the class. Most of us have had a minimum of one humiliating experience while standing with chalk dusted fingers, with the eyes of every math student piercing through us. These are the images that haunt us all the way through adulthood. But it does not mean that we cannot learn math. It just means that we could be developing a solid case of math anxiety.

But what exactly is math anxiety? It's an very strong emotional sensation of anxiety, panic, or fear that people feel when they think about or must apply their ability to understand mathematics. Sufferers of math anxiety frequently believe that they are incapable of doing activities or taking classes that involve math skills. In fact, some people with math anxiety have developed such a fear that it has become a phobia; aptly named math phobia.

The incidence of math anxiety, especially among college test takers, but also among high school test takers, has risen considerably over the last 10 years, and currently this increase shows no signs of slowing down. Frequently test takers will even chose their college majors and programs based specifically on how little math will be compulsory for the completion of the degree.

The prevalence of math anxiety has become so dramatic on college campuses that many of these schools have special counseling programs that are designed to assist math anxious test takers to deal with their discomfort and their math problems.

Math anxiety itself is not an intellectual problem, as many people have been lead to believe; it is, in fact, an emotional problem that stems from improper math teaching techniques that have slowly built and reinforced these feelings. However, math anxiety can result in an intellectual problem when its symptoms interfere with a person's ability to learn and understand math.

The fear of math can cause a sort of "glitch" in the brain that can cause an otherwise clever person to stumble over even the simplest of math problems. A study by Dr. Mark H. Ashcraft of Cleveland State University in Ohio showed that college test takers who usually perform well, but who suffer from math anxiety, will suffer from fleeting lapses in their working memory when they are asked to perform even the most basic mental arithmetic. These same issues regarding memory were not present in the same test takers when they were required to answer questions that did not involve numbers. This very clearly demonstrated that the memory phenomenon is quite specific to only math.

So what exactly is it that causes this inhibiting math anxiety? Unfortunately it is not as simple as one answer, since math anxiety doesn't have one specific cause. Frequently math anxiety can result of a student's either negative experience or embarrassment with math or a math teacher in previous years.

These circumstances can prompt the student to believe that he or she is somehow deficient in his or her math abilities. This belief will consistently lead to a poor performance in math tests and courses in general, leading only to confirm the beliefs of the student's inability. This particular phenomenon is referred to as the "self-fulfilling prophecy" by the psychological community. Math anxiety will result in poor performance, rather than it being the other way around.

Dr. Ashcraft stated that math anxiety is a "It's a learned, almost phobic, reaction to math," and that it is not only people prone to anxiety, fear, or panic who can develop math anxiety. The image alone of doing math problems can send the blood pressure and heart rate to race, even in the calmest person.

The study by Dr. Ashcraft and his colleague Elizabeth P. Kirk, discovered that test takers who suffered from math anxiety were frequently stumped by issues of even the most basic

- 99 -

math rules, such as "carrying over" a number, when performing a sum, or "borrowing" from a number when doing a subtraction. Lapses such as this occurred only on working memory questions involving numbers.

To explain the problem with memory, Ashcraft states that when math anxiety begins to take its effect, the sufferer experiences a rush of thoughts, leaving little room for the focus required to perform even the simplest of math problems. He stated that "you're draining away the energy you need for solving the problem by worrying about it."

The outcome is a "vicious cycle," for test takers who are sufferers of math anxiety. As math anxiety is developed, the fear it promotes stands in the way of learning, leading to a decrease in self-confidence in the ability to perform even simple arithmetic.

The way in which math is taught to test takers today is a large portion of the problem. In the US, test takers are frequently taught the rules of math, but rarely will they learn why a specific approach to a math problems work. Should test takers be provided with a foundation of "deeper understanding" of math, it may prevent the development of phobias.

Another study that was published in the Journal of Experimental Psychology by Dr. Jamie Campbell and Dr. Qilin Xue of the University of Saskatchewan in Saskatoon, Canada, reflected the same concepts. The researchers in this study looked at university test takers who were educated in Canada and China, discovering that the Chinese test takers could generally outperform the Canadian-educated test takers when it came to solving complex math problems involving procedural knowledge - the ability to know how to solve a math problem, instead of simply having ideas memorized.

A portion of this result seemed to be due to the use of calculators within both elementary and secondary schools; while Canadians frequently used them, the Chinese test takers did not.
However, calculators were not the only issue. Since Chinese-educated test takers also outperformed Canadian-educated test takers in complex math, it is suggested that cultural factors may also have an impact. However, the short-cut of using the calculator may hinder the development of the problem solving skills that are key to performing well in math.

Though it is critical that test takers develop such fine math skills, it is easier said than done. It would involve an overhaul of the training among all elementary and secondary educators, changing the education major in every college.

Math Myths

One problem that contributes to the progression of math anxiety, is the belief of many math myths. These erroneous math beliefs include the following:

Men are better in math than women - however, research has failed to demonstrate that there is any difference in math ability between the sexes.
There is a single best way to solve a math problem - however, the majority of math problems can be solved in a number of different ways. By saying that there is only one way to solve a math problem, the thinking and creative skills of the student are held back.

Some people have a math mind, and others do not - in truth, the majority of people have much more potential for their math capabilities than they believe of themselves.

It is a bad thing to count by using your fingers - counting by using fingers has actually shown that an understanding of arithmetic has been established.

People who are skilled in math can do problems quickly in their heads—in actuality, even math professors will review their example problems before they teach them in their classes.

The anxieties formed by these myths can frequently be perpetuated by a range of mind games that test takers seem to play with themselves. These math mind games include the following beliefs:

I don't perform math fast enough - actually everyone has a different rate at which he or she can learn. The speed of the solving of math problems is not important as long as the student can solve it.

I don't have the mind for math - this belief can inhibit a student's belief in him or herself, and will therefore interfere with the student's real ability to learn math.

I got the correct answer, but it was done the wrong way - there is no single best way to complete a math problem. By believing this, a student's creativity and overall understanding of math is hindered.

If I can get the correct answer, then it is too simple - test takers who suffer from math anxiety frequently belittle their own abilities when it comes to their math capabilities.

Math is unrelated to my "real" life - by freeing themselves of the fear of math, math anxiety sufferers are only limiting their choices and freedoms for the rest of their life.

Fortunately, there are many ways to help those who suffer from math anxiety. Since math anxiety is a learned, psychological response to doing or thinking about math that interferes with the sufferer's ability to understand and perform math, it is not at all a reflection of the sufferer's true math skills and abilities.

Helpful Strategies

Many strategies and therapies have been developed to help test takers to overcome their math anxious responses. Some of these helpful strategies include the following:

Reviewing and learning basic arithmetic principles, techniques and methods. Frequently math anxiety is a result of the experience of many test takers with early negative situations, and these test takers have never truly developed a strong base in basic arithmetic, especially in the case of multiplication and fractions. Since math is a discipline that is built on an accumulative foundation, where the concepts are built upon gradually from simpler concepts, a student who has not achieved a solid basis in arithmetic will experience difficulty in learning higher order math. Taking a remedial math course, or a short math course that focuses on arithmetic can often make a considerable difference in reducing the anxious response that math anxiety sufferers have with math.

Becoming aware of any thoughts, actions and feelings that are related to math and responses to math. Math anxiety has a different effect on different test takers. Therefore it is very important to become familiar with any reactions that the math anxiety sufferer may have about him/herself and the situation when math has been encountered. If the sufferer becomes aware of any irrational or unrealistic thoughts, it's possible to better concentrate on replacing these thoughts with more positive and realistic ones.

Find help! Math anxiety, as we've mentioned, is a learned response, that is reinforced repeatedly over a period of time, and is therefore not something that can be eliminated instantaneously. Test takers can more effectively reduce their anxious responses with the help of many different services that are readily available. Seeking the assistance of a psychologist or counselor, especially one with a specialty in math anxiety, can assist the sufferer in performing an analysis of his/her psychological response to math, as well as learning anxiety management skills, and developing effective coping strategies. Other great tools are tutors, classes that teach better abilities to take better notes in math class, and other math learning aids.

Learning the mathematic vocabulary will instantly provide a better chance for understanding new concepts. One major issue among test takers is the lack of understanding of the terms and vocabulary that are common jargon within math classes. Typically math classes will utilize words in a completely different way from the way in which they are utilized in all other subjects. Test takers easily mistake their lack of understanding the math terms with their mathematical abilities.

Learning anxiety reducing techniques and methods for anxiety management. Anxiety greatly interferes with a student's ability to concentrate, think clearly, pay attention, and remember new concepts. When these same test takers can learn to relax, using anxiety management techniques, the student can regain his or her ability to control his or her emotional and physical symptoms of anxiety that interfere with the capabilities of mental processing.

Working on creating a positive overall attitude about mathematics. Looking at math with a positive attitude will reduce anxiety through the building of a positive attitude.

Learning to self-talk in a positive way. Pep talking oneself through a positive self talk can greatly assist in overcoming beliefs in math myths or the mind games that may be played. Positive self-talking is an effective way to replace the negative thoughts - the ones that create the anxiety. Even if the sufferer doesn't believe the statements at first, it plants a positive seed in the subconscious, and allows a positive outlook to grow.

Beyond this, *test takers should learn effective math class, note taking and studying techniques.* Typically, the math anxious test takers will avoid asking questions to save themselves from embarrassment. They will sit in the back of classrooms, and refrain from seeking assistance from the professor. Moreover, they will put off studying for math until the very last moment, since it causes them such substantial discomfort. Alone, or a combination of these negative behaviors work only to reduce the anxiety of the test takers, but in reality, they are actually building a substantially more intense anxiety.

There are many different positive behaviors that can be adopted by math anxious test takers, so that they can learn to better perform within their math classes.

- Sit near the front of the class. This way, there will be fewer distractions, and there will be more of a sensation of being a part of the topic of discussion.
- If any questions arise, ASK! If one student has a question, then there are certain to be others who have the same question but are too nervous to ask - perhaps because they have not yet learned how to deal with their own math anxiety.
- Seek extra help from the professor after class or during office hours.
- Prepare, prepare, prepare - read textbook material before the class, do the homework and work out any problems available within the textbook. Math skills are developed through practice and repetition, so the more practice and repetition, the better the math skills.
- Review the material once again after class, to repeat it another time, and to reinforce the new concepts that were learned.
- Beyond these tactics that can be taken by the test takers themselves, teachers and parents need to know that they can also have a large impact on the reduction of math anxiety within test takers.

As parents and teachers, there is a natural desire to help test takers to learn and understand how they will one day utilize different math techniques within their everyday lives. But when the student or teacher displays the symptoms of a person who has had nightmarish memories regarding math, where hesitations then develop in the instruction of test takers, these fears are automatically picked up by the test takers and commonly adopted as their own.

However, it is possible for teachers and parents to move beyond their own fears to better educate test takers by overcoming their own hesitations and learning to enjoy math.

Begin by adopting the outlook that math is a beautiful, imaginative or living thing. Of course, we normally think of mathematics as numbers that can be added or subtracted, multiplied or divided, but that is simply the beginning of it.

By thinking of math as something fun and imaginative, parents and teachers can teach children different ways to manipulate numbers, for example in balancing a checkbook. Parents rarely tell their children that math is everywhere around us; in nature, art, and even architecture. Usually, this is because they were never shown these relatively simple connections. But that pattern can break very simply through the participation of parents and teachers.

The beauty and hidden wonders of mathematics can easily be emphasized through a focus that can open the eyes of test takers to the incredible mathematical patterns that arise everywhere within the natural world. Observations and discussions can be made into things as fascinating as spider webs, leaf patterns, sunflowers and even coastlines. This makes math not only beautiful, but also inspiring and (dare we say) fun!

Pappas Method

For parents and teachers to assist their test takers in discovering the true wonders of mathematics, the techniques of Theoni Pappas can easily be applied, as per her popular and celebrated book "Fractals, Googols and Other Mathematical Tales." Pappas used to be a math phobia sufferer and created a fascinating step-by-step program for parents and teachers to use in order to teach test takers the joy of math.

Her simple, constructive step-by-step program goes as follows:

Don't let your fear of math come across to your kids - Parents must be careful not to perpetuate the mathematical myth - that math is only for specially talented "math types." Strive not to make comments like; "they don't like math" or "I have never been good at math." When children overhear comments like these from their primary role models they begin to dread math before even considering a chance of experiencing its wonders. It is important to encourage your children to read and explore the rich world of mathematics, and to practice mathematics without imparting negative biases.

Don't immediately associate math with computation (counting) - It is very important to realize that math is not just numbers and computations, but a realm of exciting ideas that touch every part of our lives -from making a telephone call to how the hair grows on someone's head. Take your children outside and point out real objects that display math concepts. For example, show them the symmetry of a leaf or angles on a building. Take a close look at the spirals in a spider web or intricate patterns of a snowflake.

Help your child understand why math is important - Math improves problem solving, increases competency and should be applied in different ways. It's the same as reading. You can learn the basics of reading without ever enjoying a novel. But, where's the excitement in that? With math, you could stop with the basics. But why when there is so much more to be gained by a fuller Understanding? Life is so much more enriching when we go beyond the basics. Stretch your children's minds to become involved in mathematics in ways that will not only be practical but also enhance their lives.

Make math as "hands on" as possible - Mathematicians participate in mathematics. To really experience math encourage your child to dig in and tackle problems in creative ways. Help them learn how to manipulate numbers using concrete references they understand as well as things they can see or touch. Look for patterns everywhere, explore shapes and symmetries. How many octagons do you see each day on the way to the grocery store? Play math puzzles and games and then encourage your child to try to invent their own. And, whenever possible, help your child realize a mathematical conclusion with real and tangible results. For example, measure out a full glass of juice with a measuring cup and then ask your child to drink half. Measure what is left. Does it measure half of a cup?

Read books that make math exciting:

Fractals, Googols and Other Mathematical Tales introduces an animated cat who explains fractals, tangrams and other mathematical concepts you've probably never heard of to children in terms they can understand. This book can double as a great text book by using one story per lesson.
A Wrinkle in Time is a well-loved classic, combining fantasy and science.

The Joy of Mathematics helps adults explore the beauty of mathematics that is all around.

The Math Curse is an amusing book for 4-8 year olds.
The Gnarly Gnews is a free, humorous bi-monthly newsletter on mathematics.

The Phantom Tollbooth is an Alice in Wonderland-style adventure into the worlds of words and numbers.

Use the internet to help your child explore the fascinating world of mathematics.

Web Math provides a powerful set of math-solvers that gives you instant answers to the stickiest problems.

Math League has challenging math materials and contests for fourth grade and above.
Silver Burdett Ginn Mathematics offers Internet-based math activities for grades K-6.

The Gallery of Interactive Geometry is full of fascinating, interactive geometry activities.

Math is very much like a language of its own. And like any second language, it will get rusty if it is not practiced enough. For that reason, test takers should always be looking into new ways to keep understanding and brushing up on their math skills, to be certain that foundations do not crumble, inhibiting the learning of new levels of math.

There are many different books, services and websites that have been developed to take the fear out of math, and to help even the most uncertain student develop self confidence in his or her math capabilities.

There is no reason for math or math classes to be a frightening experience, nor should it drive a student crazy, making them believe that they simply don't have the "math brain" that is needed to solve certain problems.

There are friendly ways to tackle such problems and it's all a matter of dispelling myths and creating a solid math foundation.

Concentrate on re-learning the basics and feeling better about yourself in math, and you'll find that the math brain you've always wanted was there all along.

Additional Bonus Material

Due to our efforts to try to keep this book to a manageable length, we've created a link that will give you access to all of your additional bonus material.

Please visit http://www.mometrix.com/bonus948/wonderlicslep to access the information.